PORTFOLIO
KARMAYOGI

M.S. Ashokan is an author and senior journalist with over twenty years of experience. He currently works with the *Deshabhimani* daily. Painting (in oil and watercolour) is a passion that he pursues seriously. He lives in Kochi with his wife and two children.

Rajesh Rajamohan is a writer, translator and technologist. He lives in Pennsylvania, US, and works for the telecommunications industry. He translated N.S. Madahavn's *Litanies of Dutch Battery*, a major work from Malayalam, in 2011. The book won the Vodafone-Crossword Award for best translated fiction, was shortlisted for The Hindu Literary Prize and longlisted for the Man Asian Literary Prize. His other works of translation include K.R. Meera's *Gospel of Yudas*.

KARMAYOGI

A Biography of
E. SREEDHARAN

M.S. ASHOKAN

Translated by
RAJESH RAJAMOHAN

PORTFOLIO
PENGUIN

An imprint of Penguin Random House

PORTFOLIO

USA | Canada | UK | Ireland | Australia
New Zealand | India | South Africa | China

Portfolio is part of the Penguin Random House group of companies
whose addresses can be found at global.penguinrandomhouse.com

Published by Penguin Random House India Pvt. Ltd
4th Floor, Capital Tower 1, MG Road,
Gurugram 122 002, Haryana, India

Penguin
Random House
India

First published in Portfolio by Penguin Books India 2015

ISBN 9780143425304

Typeset in Adobe Caslon Pro by Manipal Digital Systems, Manipal
Printed at Manipal Technologies Limited, India

www.penguin.co.in

MIX
Paper from
responsible sources
FSC® C043100

Contents

Foreword

Sreedharan has become a synonym for the magnificence of human endeavour that makes the impossible possible. There has not been any parallel, in the last six decades, to his contribution as a technocrat who modernized and expanded the country's transportation systems to match global standards. What stands out about this genius, who hails from Karukaputhur, an obscure, remote village in the district of Palakkad in Kerala, is not just the sheer volume and reach of the development projects he undertook, but also how in mission after mission, he reaffirmed the time-tested values from ancient wisdom that he has always cherished, functioning with purpose and transparency even while keeping corruption at bay, with an effort akin to prayer.

The nation took note of Sreedharan, the trailblazer, when he led the epic mission of building the Konkan Railway on a tight schedule to link the northern end of Kerala—the southernmost state of India—to the financial city of Mumbai. Known as one of the greatest engineering feats of modern times, the Konkan line ran along the west coast of India, negotiating the difficult terrain that lay between the Western Ghats and the Arabian Sea. That a railway line boosts a region's industrial and economic prospects had long been realized, and plans for such a line had been in the making since the time of the British Raj. However, all attempts to implement them came to naught, what with the Konkan's forbidding terrain making it a terribly impractical prospect—that is, until Sreedharan took charge.

Sreedharan had long retired from the Indian Railways when parleys for the country's first modern metro in Delhi began and his name was suggested for heading the project. There were legal barriers to appointing a retiree in the top position at a public enterprise. However, no argument or obstruction could thwart Sreedharan's progress along his path of action for very long. The Sreedharan Effect extended beyond the Delhi Metro; following its success twenty more big cities in India embarked on plans for metros of their own.

The new transportation system that would come with an incredibly steep price tag, one which the country could hardly afford, drew prolonged and intense criticism. But in the end, the success of the metro in Delhi, which flaunted the most advanced technology from around the world, made for a fitting reply to all the naysayers. The benefits the metro brought—such as significant reduction in pollution, decline in road accidents, improved infrastructure that accelerated development activities, and change in the quality of life of the general public—blunted much of the criticism. What was more, efforts had begun to expand public transportation projects by inviting private participation. But Sreedharan openly rejected this idea. He contended that ownership and operation by the government was the only reason for the success of projects of the metro kind, proving beneficial to the people while remaining growth-oriented.

Sreedharan does not possess the halo of the IIT graduate or a Civil Services luminary considered among the holy cows of India. Armed with only a regular degree in civil engineering, Sreedharan's success lay in his unflinching commitment to his core values in both his personal and professional lives. This commitment took him on an incredible ascent to the pinnacle of achievement in his field. His philosophy of committed and ethical work would stand taller than the gargantuan projects delivered under his groundbreaking engineering and management brilliance. The Bhagavad Gita had always been his inspiration. Having—as he describes it—imbibed the supreme power of motivation from the book that 'cracks open the path of action for the seeker', Sreedharan would always share the Gita's message with his colleagues.

This book is an attempt to get up and close to the man and his life that have inspired many, including the younger generations. He has magnanimously given his precious time to the author despite his singularly hectic professional life, graciously ironed out factual kinks, adding relevant clarity from start to finish. Here is hoping this modest tribute will help readers get a closer glimpse of the genius the nation has come to love, admire and even revere in their hearts and minds.

The Story of Sreedharan

8 January 2013, Kochi

Before the day broke, a clutch of OB vans from assorted news channels made a beeline for the hotel Le Meridien. The heated debates livening up the Malayalee NRI conference at the convention centre revolved around one question— would Delhi Metro Rail Corporation (DMRC) and E. Sreedharan be leading the much-awaited Kochi Metro project? Union Minister for Urban Development Kamal Nath, Chief Minister of Kerala Oommen Chandy and four other central ministers from Kerala were cooped up in the hotel, tasked with making the all-important and final decision on DMRC's role in the project. Updates from correspondents flew from the Le Meridien to the news channels minute by minute. The breaking news scroll on the channels ran a different story every couple of minutes.

Into this charged atmosphere—thick with the fog of disputes that had raged for months and that were now headed to their climax—the principal advisor for DMRC,

E. Sreedharan, was making his way in. His car rolled into the convention centre and he stepped out of it, his face bearing his usual solemn expression, divulging little of what was on his mind. Those who were looking to interpret something from his body language were disappointed. The meeting continued behind closed doors, while outside, newsmen indulged themselves in a fresh wave of speculation.

It was all over in just half an hour! Everyone came out of the centre at the same time. Sreedharan's face still revealed nothing. The central minister announced to an army of newspersons that they had decided to go with DMRC and Sreedharan for the metro project. Sreedharan forced a smile as this much-anticipated news was announced. Yet, there was no triumph in his voice when he talked to journalists afterwards, although the decision had been a hard-fought victory that took over a year. His demeanour appeared to proclaim that everything had happened just as it should have, whereas those who announced the decision were bending over backwards to make it look to the media that there really was no choice other than DMRC and Sreedharan.

Anybody who followed the Kochi Metro project's timeline would know that the story was quite the opposite. It involved a fight that kicked up quite a dust. There were both open and unseen machinations to put DMRC and Sreedharan out of the contest. In Sreedharan's absence, public perception was of graft where crores of rupees changed hands in the name of commissions in an unholy alliance, as elements with vested interests in the government and state leadership planted themselves behind the challengers. In the end, the will of those who had determined to bring Sreedharan into the project's leadership prevailed, thwarting the opposition emphatically. Sreedharan himself asked for no quarter and fought his battles alone, but his fight was never that of a loner. Without even a single call to action from him, the public and the media had rallied behind him to make sure that the Kochi Metro would not become another basket case of corruption.

It was curiously noted that Sreedharan had never uttered a word in public against his detractors. He would repeat his message firmly, as befitting a battle-wise warrior, in his inimitable style: he merely wanted to finish the project without delay and without corruption, simply for the benefit of the people. The plotters had no choice but to beat a retreat, admitting defeat. Those who wrote off Sreedharan as just another project manager or a civil engineer capable of executing big projects were handed a loud and clear message that his name had found its way into the hearts and minds of the people at large, and could not be dismissed.

Sreedharan's accomplishments, starting from the construction of the Pampan Bridge, to the execution of the Konkan Railway and the Delhi Metro, had given him the image of a superhuman in the hearts of the masses. They have brought him the kind of fame and appreciation hitherto commanded only by Bollywood stars or cricket gods. But that alone could not guarantee that he would pull off the kind of miracles that he had done every time, the Kochi Metro being the latest. Could we even hazard an assertion that we could not ever incubate a greater enterprise in the country than the Konkan Railways project, which billed thousands of crores of rupees? Wouldn't there be a time when Sreedharan's recipe of engineering skills and technology, which had given birth to the metros across Kolkata (also Calcutta), Delhi and Kochi (also Cochin), goes out of date? Wouldn't there be a time too for amazing dams and express highways, at the expense of the millions of impoverished taxpayers who would be displaced out of their domicile and commercial properties in the name of development? Weren't the Indian cities going to get closer to each other on either side of time's straight line in bullet trains blazing through underground tunnels and scaffoldings in the sky?

What explains Sreedharan's popularity? No doubt there are excellent engineers and project managers in the country who have assimilated the latest and superior technologies, and are as good as the best anywhere in the world, capable of shaping up impossible glories. What is special about Sreedharan, then?

What talisman does he possess to in turn possess the hearts and minds of the people close to him? Why would the public and media accord a civil engineer from a small village in Kerala their greatest admiration and approval, a phenomenon that typically belongs in the realm of mass leaders? Google 'E. Sreedharan' and the search returns more than five million results. You will find a Wikipedia page on Sreedharan, which gives you brief biographical sketches of him. There are Facebook profiles on him created by unknown fans from distant corners of the country. There are innumerable YouTube videos streaming his convocation speeches at IITs and the many interviews he granted to national news channels. There are forums passionately urging the government not to delay their deliberations to confer the ultimate civilian recognition for an Indian, the Bharat Ratna, on Sreedharan. You could not even begin to count the number of blogs in many different languages celebrating the Metro Man. There are travelogues and diaries written by passengers who have travelled on the Konkan tracks or the Delhi Metro, talking about not just the conveniences in terms of time and money that the new lines have brought them, but expressing grateful praise for the new vistas that are now open to them. Hundreds of pictures, caricatures and cartoons relating to Sreedharan abound on the Internet. There is an Internet edition of a picture book on Sreedharan's epic career, uploaded by a private publisher from Mumbai (also Bombay); DMRC's chief public relations officer Anuj Dayal's book *Delhi Metro Gatha* is on sale in online bookshops; there are numerous audio and video archives of every word uttered by Sreedharan to the media, and testimonials on him from prominent management gurus and nation builders. Sreedharan held the public in thrall even at the age of eighty. As if this isn't enough, state governments clamour to get Sreedharan at the helm for all their big-ticket projects. Private corporations, of course, would love to have him in any position and at any price. Sreedharan, feted by the nation with the Padma Shri and the Padma Bhushan awards, continues to get awards and recognitions almost every day, from both within the country and overseas.

By the year 2014, Sreedharan the technocrat had spent sixty years in the public space. He had joined the Indian Railways Engineering Service (IRES) as an assistant engineer in 1954, and retired from the organization after thirty-six years of service in 1990. He founded Konkan Rail Corporation Limited (KRCL), spending seven years there, after which he became the managing director of DMRC in 1997. When he retired from DMRC in December 2011, he was seventy-nine years of age. At that time, having spent fifty-seven years in public service, all he wanted was a quiet life in retirement. However, he was given the task of overseeing the Kochi Metro, the monorails in Kozhikode and Thiruvananthapuram, and the construction of the south-west speed-rail track right away. He took on these new challenges at eighty-one with the same earnestness that he had displayed six decades earlier when he walked into the Indian Railways, re-embarking on a work life of non-stop travel, moving between Ponnani, Kochi, Thiruvananthapuram, New Delhi and Bengaluru (also Bangalore).

The projects Sreedharan undertook to deliver, from the Pampan Bridge to the Kochi Metro, involved about Rs 10 lakh crore in investments. Not one of them was sullied by even a hint of corruption. One saw tens of lakhs of rupees change hands even in janitorial contracts for the Commonwealth Games. It was as part of the city's preparations for the same event that the Delhi Metro's second phase was completed; it needed a whopping

Rs 24,000 crore. Sreedharan oversaw the task. When the Commonwealth Games corruption scandal snared even central ministers in jail, the Delhi Metro was the only project that emerged without blemish.

Sreedharan left the Indian Railways with the wealth of three and a half decades of accomplishments in civil engineering, having finished enormous missions. The construction and renovation of all major rail lines, and their doubling, were completed during his time with the railways, and he played a large part in it. But Sreedharan came to the world's notice after his reconstruction of the Pampan Bridge in record time after a storm surge struck the island. He boarded a Rameswaram-bound train in 1964 with a mission to reconstruct the bridge, which used to be known as a British engineering marvel. He was only thirty-one. What Sreedharan termed as a triumph of engineering was completed in only forty-six days—a mere half of the estimated time. That night, when the then railway minister S.K. Patil announced that the project would be completed in a week's time, Sreedharan had already installed the last girder in the bridge to flag off the first train towards the shores of Rameswaram.

Sreedharan's next major mission was the design of the Calcutta Metro (now Kolkata Metro), which was to become the model for modern national public transportation systems in India. The Indian Railways ventured into the project with minimal knowhow or understanding of metro rail systems, as did Sreedharan. He accepted the daunting tasks of designing and planning the project.

Paying for himself, he spent four days studying the Tokyo Metro lines; the result of this was a world-class metro rail system in Kolkata that runs entirely underground. As for Sreedharan, his appetite to learn did not end with this engineering feat. Although he was not responsible for the lapses in the build and delivery processes at Kolkata, he was resolute in making sure they never happened again in his future enterprises.

He could have been successful anywhere, and not just with railway-related projects. His stint as chairman and managing director of Cochin Shipyard illustrated this. Never did that institution have such an exceptional leader. He was there for just a year, and had to overcome the malaise of endemic negativity among the trade unions in bringing out the yard's first-ever ship, *Rani Padmini*. It was a remarkable success and a proud moment for the country. Along the way, he publicly exposed the unholy nexus between the bureaucrats and administrators who were the actual beneficiaries of commissions in crores of rupees from foreign purchases. This singular act displayed the stamp of distinction that was Sreedharan's, and was an early sign of the professionalism and tenacity that he displayed throughout his career.

The Konkan project, an epic in the history of the Indian Railways, followed next. The scale and range of challenges Sreedharan had to overcome in order to build 760 kilometres of track, starting from Mangalore in the south to the town of Roha in Maharashtra in the west, were immense and hard, to say the least. The track would run between the restless Arabian Sea and the Western Ghats that stood tall facing the sea. The project, which had wilted away in the archives after having been written off as an impossible task since the time of the British, took only seven years and three months to complete under Sreedharan's leadership. He systematically and doggedly wiped out every single obstacle in its path. It was the treacherous terrain, and not money for the gigantic construction, that posed the challenge. Not only did the tracks run through the difficult terrains of four states, the stretch had to negotiate the more difficult task of handling four incompatible and paradoxical political systems. With his inimitable skills of diplomacy, Sreedharan broke through all resistance—geological and political—stringing along everyone in laying out the engineering miracle.

Having spent four decades on official duty by the time the Konkan mission was done, Sreedharan was preparing to put his feet up. By then, DMRC was established for the Delhi Metro project. Sreedharan, originally on the committee appointed to scout for a managing director, found himself appointed for the job. In the initial period, he shouldered both responsibilities—the Konkan Railway and the Delhi Metro—shuttling between Mumbai and Delhi without respite. What amazed the people of Delhi was not just the construction of the most modern metro line, but the attention taken every step of the way to make sure that the everyday life of the citizens was not affected. The mission progressed at great speed and, notably, without impacting the environment. In just two years and nine months, the first phase of the Delhi Metro was completed, three months earlier than originally scheduled, and without cost overruns of even a single rupee above the estimated Rs 10,500 crore. The project's 124-kilometre second phase, projected to cost Rs 24,000 crore and estimated to lose Rs 2.5 crore every single day of delay, took only four and a half years to commission. In the annals of metro development projects, it was indeed a world record.

Let us reflect for a minute to put all these achievements in perspective: they happened in a nation where building a simple, functional bridge or a narrow road in a panchayat generally costs tens of lakhs of rupees and happens at such an excruciatingly slow pace as to be of little real benefit.

However, Sreedharan would dismiss the attribution of his accomplishments to any superhuman gift he may have. His standard response to queries on which was the greater of his masterpieces, the Konkan line or the Delhi Metro, would be 'neither'. The most important achievement, he would say, was that our engineers were instilled with a self-confidence that enabled them to work competently. These engineers came from modest backgrounds and did not have a pedigree education, proving that all they needed was the backing of people such as Sreedharan to produce world-class work.

Sreedharan would always emphasize that the value system he had adopted at work as well as on the personal front was the foundation for his success. The two organizations he built from ground up—Konkan Railway Corporation and Delhi Metro Rail Corporation—were in striking contrast to the traditional ideas of a public enterprise, as discerning observers could see. DMRC became so well known, it was looked up to by private corporations, and management students from all over the world, including Stanford University and London University, descended on the Corporation to study the institution and its business values. Sreedharan revealed his magic mantras at their behest: be honest in your private and public life in such a way that you don't need to try hard to convince anybody; stand firm and do not cede an inch while discharging your duties with conviction; polish your professional skills and do not let it go out of date; keep your integrity so you hold in esteem even the most downtrodden in the society in your plans; be moral; follow habits that rejuvenate both your body and mind.

Sreedharan had been in the Indian Railways for thirty-six years, of which the first fifteen saw him pack up and move twenty-five times. He was subjected to constant job transfers, but that did not stop him from consistently making it to the leadership of major projects. There were a fair number of people who found his honesty and inflexibility quite annoying, but they could not mount a challenge to him as they came up against the unassailable wall of his professionalism and technical excellence. According to Sreedharan, honesty is not a state where corruption is absent, but actively taking a stand to benefit the institution and society for the long term.

Not many knew that Sreedharan would not spend a minute beyond eight hours at work. His work hours started at nine in the morning, an hour for the lunch break and ended at six in the evening. He never took a single file home, even during his time at DMRC, where the many dauntingly complex cases demanded resolution of multiple issues at the same time. The technocrat, who would go deep into the taxing chores of his day job and is frequently out on hectic travels, transforms into another person at home. He would ease into the role of the elderly patriarch, narrating stories from the epics and the Puranas to the children at home. Until a couple of years ago, he had worked in all corners of the country. Yet, he took his family along each time, facing great odds. He would advise his colleagues that the family needed to be together at all costs.

Sreedharan is a staunch proponent and a tireless advocate of the value of a professional's social commitment as the driver of development. To his engineering students, he would say that their acquiring knowledge of new technologies and putting them to use for the common good would be the fondest gift for their teacher.

While diligently adhering to the protocols of official life, Sreedharan unleashed his biting criticism of wayward bureaucracy, whenever opportunity called for it. He openly said that those who could not make useful decisions were a negative influence on the nation's progress, and that they were not really interested in doing anything to begin with. His comment—'the sole intent here seemed to be to block anyone who wanted to do something worthwhile'—was directed at those who argued against the Delhi Metro project during its nascent stages. His warning that it would cost taxpayers Rs 1.4 crore for every day of delay hit the spot. The Indian Administrative Service (IAS) officers who had made disapproving noises bore the brunt of Sreedharan's scathing reproaches. He argued that it was too technical and complex a project for IAS officers to be able to micromanage it on the strength of their administrative skills alone. A Chief Secretary, who had opposed the project from start to finish, even after the central government and the state government of Delhi had taken the final decision on it, was also a target of Sreedharan's censure.

Sreedharan would not let the political leadership have their way and compromise the project for selfish gains. He was not scared of vendetta for his stinging criticism of political blockades over the metro project when they took a turn for the worse. He looked the political gods in the eye and remarked that he could only see politicians there, no nation builders. What goes on is not governing, but demeaning political gamesmanship.

Seated at the top position in DMRC, a public organization with equal participation of the state and central governments, Sreedharan observed and commented boldly on institutional corruption and the black money Mafiosi. He believes that government workers are susceptible to graft because of the proliferation of black money, which has taken deep root in the society and has created this situation, and not because they do not earn enough. There are laws to rein in the corrupt, and police to enforce the laws. But the police themselves are corrupt. There have been bills passed to reform the police force, but they are not implemented even when the Supreme Court demanded it. That should mean the real culprits are the political leadership, says Sreedharan candidly. His views remind us of the death of Satyendra Dubey, which brought the public spotlight on the vocation of civil engineering. The brave engineer sacrificed his own life for his ideals while in the line of duty building the national highway. Sreedharan's policy of going against the wishes of the corrupt in politics and administration only underscores the martyrdom of Dubey's death.

The regular stream of awards and citations coming Sreedharan's way embodies the admiration and respect accorded to him by society. It started in 1965 with the first award of Rs 500 from the railway minister. The Padma Shri and Padma Vibhushan have also come his way. By the year 2013, he was honoured with more than a dozen doctoral degrees from national and international universities across the globe. He has already received more than sixty national and international awards. Each time, he would remind the audience that he was the one who had received the recognition, but that the accolades should actually go to all the colleagues who had worked with him on his projects. He channels the money from these awards into charity works, and also uses it to finance the education of students of poor means.

Sreedharan swears by his inspiration, the Bhagavad Gita. His favourite leader of the people was former chief minister of Kerala E.K. Nayanar, who was a communist. He loved the innocence of Nayanar's demeanour and the trusting brotherhood he exhibited while showing, at the same time, political steel in overcoming obstacles in his path. Sreedharan's love for the Gita begins with its message of summoning the full potential of human gifts to do selfless actions for the good of everyone. He underlines his conviction that the book is not just meant for the followers of a particular religion. The standard gift from Sreedharan to his colleagues is a copy of the Gita. However, Sreedharan does not like overt display of religion, though he is a man of faith himself. The faithful Sreedharan, sporting a sandalwood mark on his forehead, reading the epics, Puranas and the Upanishads, can only be seen in his home or in private settings with his family members. He consciously avoids all such symbols and images in his office and at formal occasions. He follows the official dress code, like his colleagues. He is unwavering in his policy to keep public spaces secular.

As soon as he retired from DMRC, top-notch corporations in India approached Sreedharan with offers that would lure just about anyone. A major enterprise sweetened the pot, asking him to name any position and offered a remuneration no less than Rs 20 lakh a month. None of these offers could bridge the distance Sreedharan kept from for-profit institutions throughout his life. Nothing could lure him to reassess his determination to live the rest of his life on his pension from the Indian Railways. Even in the years leading up to his retirement from full-time work, he would not take a rupee from the DMRC salary, which was entirely pledged to charity.

Religion, for Sreedharan, is being in the thick of action without concerning oneself with personal gains; it is about finding out what is best for the common good and submitting oneself to its fulfilment with great responsibility and excellence. He sends the message by living exactly such a life. The epithet Karmayogi describes nothing more than the essence of his spirit. He has scaled the pinnacle in his professional career, discharged his duties towards his family and, above all, kept healthy habits and his integrity as a person—indeed, he is an amalgamation of actions and qualities that make for an impeccable human being. He has the weakest of the weak members of society factored in when he handles projects worth hundreds of crores. This is the reason why a large number of lay people rally proudly behind him as he stands tall, like Arjuna on the side of righteousness in the many battles of Kurukshetra. He would not hurt anyone with word or deed, and was a calming presence and a towering source of hope for many. He insists that all his accomplishments belong not to him, but to the common people who are the real stakeholders in all his endeavours. You could read the distilled essence of his life's journey from the Yoga Vasishta Ramayan quote framed in his office:

Karyam karomi, Na kinchit aham karomi (I perform the deed. But I am not the one who does it.)

We do have government leaderships sadly hitting new lows, making money even when they procure coffins for dead soldiers who sacrificed their lives to protect the nation. Every day, we hear news of backroom bargains involving unethical and illegal commissions in return for purchase of dysfunctional defence equipment from shady dealers. Corruption being the norm of our times, what surprise then if the people adore someone who has actually delivered projects of benefit to them? Through his selfless toil, founded on moral consciousness, Sreedharan reminds us of an exalted but forgotten civilization that is our heritage. His call to action for the new generation is another quote from the Gita:

Gyanam, Param Balam
Nahi Jnanena sadrusham pavitram iha vidyate

He cannot stress enough why public servants must adhere to idealistic principles like the *suktas* from the Buddha, as they discharge their duties.

I was about to take leave of Sreedharan, having come to the end of my meeting with him at the DMRC office in Kochi, when his public relations officer, Narayanan, walked into the office hurriedly. He let Sreedharan know that there were a couple of visitors waiting outside to meet him—a father and his son. They had come with no appointment. But they were here asking for only a few minutes of his time. Narayanan was told that the son had got a job in an engineering firm. The young man, who had brought along his father who had retired from the railways, was here to ask for Sreedharan's blessings before he started his career, Narayanan explained. I thanked Sreedharan for granting me an hour and a half of his time for the interview, and stepped out of his office. I saw the father and son waiting outside the door. I could read what was written in the eyes of the young engineer, looking hopeful about his future, and the world-weary father. They were here to meet a magnetic personality, a nation's pride, a man who fetched much reverence and adulation.

The Charms of Childhood

Karukaputhur's beauty is typical of villages in the district of Palakkad in Kerala. If you travel from Pattambi to Guruvayoor by road, turn left at an intersection, aptly named Koottupatha[1] and a 5-kilometre ride will see you in Karukaputhur. Another kilometre on a narrow road across a lush-green stretch flanked by old, traditional homes will bring you to the entrance of a property with a house tucked in the middle of its expanse. You will see a little board on which is inscribed the name of the house, 'Kalliparambu'. You proceed along a dirt road flanked by coconut trees and cultivated fields on either side, getting a whiff of wet soil, on your way to the grand traditional manor—called 'Naalukettu'—standing tall in front of you. The beautiful, two-storeyed house lies at the centre of ten acres of land. Built with the sturdiest of timber, the mansion has seen more than a hundred years, but its beauty, as a representation of the solemn charm

---

[1] Intersecting roads.

of Kerala architecture, is not diminished at all, thanks to the timely repairs that have mended the ravages of time. Elattuvalappil Sreedharan was born in this stately 'Naalukettu'.

As you step into the house, you get the strong suggestion that it is suffused with the same propriety and decorum that Sreedharan follows in his personal and professional life. The massive yard and house are kept clean and orderly. Sreedharan lives in Ponnani with his wife—only an hour away from his ancestral house, which he visits at least three times every month. There are three or four domestic helps responsible for the upkeep of the house and its yard. His nephews handle matters related to the expenditure and income from farming activities on the land. Sreedharan had spent a long time away from the house for his studies and career, and looked forward to living there again when he retired from DMRC. For many reasons, however, that did not happen. Until recently, his sister and family lived here, but after her death, nobody has been living in the house. However, arrangements are made every day for any of his dear and near who may visit for a stay. Having been born here, and having grown up as the youngest among his siblings, Sreedharan has preserved a bond with the house. In the courtyard, there are pictures of the elders of the house and of his sister, who was very close to him. Adjoining the courtyard lie the puja room and the kitchen. Sreedharan pulls out a chair to the porch and sits there, introducing his neighbourhood and the family. Afterwards, he sets out for a walk in the open space around the house, familiar to him since childhood, and steps into a world of memories that linger in the house.

Sreedharan's father, Keezhoottil Neelakantan Moosathu, was a wealthy Brahmin. This house, referred to as his ancestral home, belonged to his mother, Elattu Valappil Kartyayini (Ammalu Amma). When Sreedharan was a child, though, things weren't going very well financially. His father would occasionally visit, but never really knew the plight of the family. The household used to be run by his uncles, his mother's brothers. Although they had lands, they had almost no money and had hit rock-bottom.

Sreedharan had only heard about this difficult period from his mother. His father came to know of the family's situation rather late when, one day, he visited and was shocked to see Sreedharan's mother huddled with the children, crying inconsolably. She had nothing at home and there was nothing to feed the children. When he realized how badly off they were, he asked them to pack up and leave at once with him for Nariri, where he lived in an 'Illam', a Brahmins' enclave. His father was quite well off, with farmlands and income from other properties. As a Brahmin, he could not have lived with his family in the 'Illam', according to the tradition of that time. A Brahmin was allowed to have a relationship with a woman from a Nair family, but not legal marriage with her. The custom would not allow him to settle down in his partner's home either. Respecting traditions, his father built a new house called 'Madom' in a big piece of land which was only at a shouting distance from his mother's 'Naalukettu'.

'Madom' is still around. Though Sreedharan is not very close to his father's extended family, he visits their house on all important occasions and is attentive to their needs.

The family began to flourish after Sreedharan's mother returned to Kalliparambu with the children in tow. Their father now took care of all their needs directly.

Sreedharan was born as the youngest son to Neelakantan Moosathu and Ammalu Amma on 12 June 1932. He had six brothers and two sisters. Narayani was the eldest. She was also called Ammukkutty Amma. She was about twenty years older to Sreedharan, and took care of all his needs like a mother. Krishna Menon was the next child; he too had a father-like affection for Sreedharan, and it was he who advised him on his studies and career. He took the lead in arranging Sreedharan's marriage too. This brother was an electrical engineer, and had worked in Tamil Nadu Electricity Board (TNEB) and Bombay Electric Supply Transport (BEST) before joining the reputed Alagappa Chettiyar Polytechnic in Palakkad as its principal. He later retired from the polytechnic to lead a quiet life in Palakkad. He is now no more. The third sibling was Padmanabha Menon. He had retired as a superintendent engineer from the Military Engineer Services to make Chennai (also Madras) his permanent residence. The fourth, Narayanan, was an officer in an oil company in Bahrain. As soon as he completed his basic education, he went overseas, landing a well-paying job in the Middle East. After retirement, he bought a house close to the Kerala Kala Mandalam—a centre for classical arts—in Cheruthuruthy and settled there. He too has passed away, but his wife still lives in Cheruthuruthy, where Sreedharan visits her often.

Sreedharan's only living brother is Govindan, who retired as the director of Bharatiya Vidya Bhavan, the legendary educational institution founded by K.M. Munshi. Govindan lives next to the Vishnu temple in Tripunithura. Sreedharan visits his brother at least once a week, as his position of consulting officer for the Kochi Metro requires him to be in that city often. Kesavan, another brother, younger to Govindan, had been living in Thrissur with his family, having retired from a chemical factory in Mumbai where he had found a job after he completed his bachelor's degree in commerce. The last of his brothers was Karunakaran, who had married Sreedharan's wife's older sister. He had worked as an officer with Hindustan Lever in Mumbai. Parukkutty, the youngest of his sisters, had died young from typhoid in Koyilandy, where the older sister Ammukkutty lived.

By the time Sreedharan was born, his family's financial situation had improved for good. Yet, they led a simple life, the memory of their difficult times being all too alive. Sreedharan's father was a stickler for rules and conventions, and made it a point that his children assimilated them in their everyday lives. He focused on imparting a good education to his children. It was his view that education would hold his children in good stead through their lives, more than any material wealth passed on to them. Govindan remembers their father repeat this every so often. The children grew up being responsible and loyal to the family. There was a two-to-three-year age gap between each sibling and the next. The older children, who had had a good education, found jobs and took care of the family, seeing to the education and careers of the younger ones. Their mother was involved deeply in their well-being. Possibly on account of the hardships and adversities she had been through, she displayed kindness and generosity to everyone. She made sure all visitors to her home were provided with at least two meals a day. A reserve of food was always kept aside for the unexpected guest.

The brothers did well in academics. Sreedharan remembers fondly the story of how his brother Govindan became a chartered accountant. After finishing his bachelor's in commerce, Govindan was given Rs 250 by his father, who suggested that it was time he learnt to support himself, as resources had to be found to educate the younger children who were still in school. Govindan boarded a train to Bombay with the money. He found an accountant's job there with a salary of Rs 150. Part of the money he saved was spent on his chartered accountancy studies and the rest was sent to the family every month. He had to endure great difficulties to manage this. The money he sent was used to educate a younger child; each brother proceeded to do the same.

Govindan remembers how Sreedharan was an exceptional student in school. Sreedharan used to play football. He did not join any of the clubs near his home though. He would come home from school and get busy with chores around the house, enthusiastically feeding the cows and watering the garden. He would do any job in good time, and judiciously. In the evening he would chant prayers. Being the youngest, he was showered with love and care. His oldest sister Ammukkutty Amma would bathe and dress him for school when he was very young. She would be the one to take him through his lessons in the higher grades too.

Chathannoor Government Lower Primary was Sreedharan's elementary school where he studied till fourth grade. He would walk about 4 kilometres to school every day. When he was a very small lad, someone from the house would carry him all the way, but soon he began to walk to school with his brothers. The century-old school had operated on Sreedharan's family property in a place called Mathuppally. When the reformist youth from the neighbourhood decided to start a new school, they faced many problems, foremost among which was finding a suitable location for it. Realizing the need of the times, Sreedharan's family gave up their land for the new school. The school, which began in a modest building, flourished, and later moved to another place where it could continue its expansion. Sreedharan studied in the new school.

Sreedharan was the chief guest at the centenary celebrations of the school. He donated Rs 3 lakh to the school. Along with his wife Radha, he returned again to the school last year, their intent being to pass on some award money he had received in New Delhi recently. The children, their teachers, their parents and community leaders flocked to the school to meet him. His face was flush with, perhaps, memories of his student years when he took a stroll down the entire length of the school, going back seventy years in time. He could make out the new additions to the school building, and recalled some of the names of his teachers and fellow students.

He was dismayed at the school's present condition. He pointed to the perilously disintegrating roof, and spent hours discussing renovation plans with the teachers and the parents in great detail. He returned, promising another Rs 3 lakh in funds. The headmistress of the school revealed that Sreedharan had sent Rs 10,000 to the school every year for a very long time. Additionally, Sreedharan sponsors one child's education at the school, she said.

Once Sreedharan finished primary school, there was the question of where he would go for his high school education. There were no high schools near Sreedharan's home, and the nearest one in Kumaranellur was about 20 kilometres away. One could not travel that far every day. The solution was for Sreedharan to stay with his sister's family in Koyilandy. Her husband, who worked in the Kozhikode sub-registrar's office, had rented a house nearby. The sister said Sreedharan could stay with her and go to the nearby school where her children were enrolled too. Once he began to live in Koyilandy, Sreedharan practically lost touch with his ancestral home in Karukaputhur. It became a vacation haunt for him. Even after joining the railways, he never got back to being an everyday member of the house.

Sreedharan began to live with his sister's family. He joined fifth grade in a government school in the neighbourhood. It was at this time that he met the man who was the greatest influence in his life. The values and practices followed in the family he lived with shaped the core of his character, he says. His sister's husband, Narayana Menon, personified healthy habits and hard work. He worked for the government, but was untouched by the unethical practices that were almost the custom for the average public servant. At the registration office, which was notorious for corruption, he was known for his high integrity. He was not well off, but he worked hard to raise an extended family on his meagre salary. Sreedharan admired his brother-in-law for his strength of character, which was to leave a deep impression on him and became for him a model to emulate. Later in his life, when he was confronted with the rotten and deviant culture of corruption among public officials at close quarters, he would feel proud of his association with his brother-in-law. Sreedharan vouches for his family's role in moulding the person he became. Both his mother and father hailed from powerful and wealthy families in the region. However, despite the comfort and aloofness of their privileged life, the families were in touch with the common people, who were always welcome to seek their help. Sreedharan's generation too had continued the tradition.

Sreedharan had spent more time with his sister's family than with his parents. He had to live with her family in order to attend school. Once, when he was in sixth grade, he was struck by a painful bout of psoriasis. He found he could not get out of the house after the half-yearly exams. It became clear that there was going to be a break in the academic year, having been house-bound for months. Though he could not appear for the final examinations, his academic excellence was favourably considered to promote him to seventh grade. It was during this time that Parukkutty, the other sister who was in eighth grade, and also staying with Sreedharan at their sister's, contracted typhoid and passed away. A little later, Narayana Menon got transferred to Palakkad.

One of the memories from his school years in Koyilandy was the close view he would get of trains passing by on a track which he had to cross on his way to school. He would marvel at the spectacle, and the speed with which they passed captivated him. He would walk up to the engine of the train whenever one was at a halt on the tracks, and take a close look at it. Sreedharan remembers it was not just the regular, fleeting charm a child would have for a large, random machine.

Sreedharan later moved, along with the sister's family, to Palakkad, to a place called Kotta Maithanam. He joined Basel Evangelical Mission High School to continue studies, and finished his final year there. After his retirement from the railways, Sreedharan took part in the 150th annual celebration of the school as its chief guest. He gave away Rs 3 lakh as unsolicited donation for purchase of academic materials for the students. Later, when the school needed funds for renovation, Sreedharan took the lead to collect Rs 8 lakh to express his gratitude to his alma mater.

One of Sreedharan's classmates from the Mission High School became a top bureaucrat in India. The nation knew him as a Cabinet Secretary and the grand facilitator of political churning in India as the country's chief election commissioner. If T.N. Seshan was known to the world for his stubbornness as a hawkish enforcer of rules and regulations, Sreedharan knew only a mild-mannered and pleasant fellow student who was focused completely on academics. Sreedharan and Seshan forged a friendship from the very beginning of their time at school. From Sreedharan's account, you could not find the Seshan who had filled the news with his brash retorts, his obduracy and his habitual nose for controversies. Sreedharan was involved in a few activities like football and the Boy Scouts group. Seshan had no time for any of this and concentrated on his studies. He would go home as soon as school was over. He did not make many friends. He had a great command over English, which impressed everyone including Sreedharan.

After finishing school, Sreedharan and Seshan joined Victoria College in Palakkad to pursue what was then called the intermediate college course. India became an independent nation when Sreedharan was in tenth grade. He distinctly recalls the great rumble of those times, although he was not part of it. No one from his family was in politics. The groundswell of the freedom movement had reached Palakkad and its neighbourhood too. However, the family was hardly in a position to put themselves in any struggle bigger than their own fight for survival. Sreedharan too ended up not being part of the national struggle. But he remembers the time when Mahatma Gandhi came to speak at Kotta Maithanam. He had joined the crowds to hear him.

The First Train Journey

Sreedharan cannot ever forget his first train ride. It was from Pattambi to Payyannur. There was not the bustling chaos of the present times at the stations then. Holding on to his father's hand, the six-year-old stepped into a new world with wonder and curiosity in his eyes as he boarded the train. He was on his way to his sister's home in Koyilandy. He was full of exhilaration as he trained his eyes and ears to each sound and view that came his way on that journey. The steam engine's fascinating body, the bogeys made of wood, the custom designed seats, the clamour, the smoke, the clouds of dust that the train raised, the wind blowing in through the outsized windows, and the passengers . . . everything became an object of wonder on that unforgettable journey. Sreedharan still remembers how he barely blinked during the ride. The memory of his first train ride never faded away.

Sreedharan still prefers trains for long journeys if he can help it. One does not experience the tranquillity of the train journey in any other means of travel. The train is the best place to be to read, to immerse oneself in thoughts, to sleep, or to simply rest. Sreedharan had devised many enjoyable ways to pass the time on his journeys. He especially liked to watch fellow passengers enter and exit trains, and simply savour the mundane, everyday railway sights that caught his attention. These days, as he is in charge of the Kochi Metro project, he relies heavily on commuter trains to get from Ponnani to Kochi and Thiruvananthapuram.

Sreedharan, who rewrote the destiny of the nation's public transportation system, made his first ever train journey in 1938. His fascination for trains during his school days might have sprung from the thrill of this first ride. He was particularly fortunate at that time for his encounter with trains. What is now known as Kerala used to consist of the three provinces of Travancore, Kochi and Malabar, and had railway infrastructure only in the Malabar. Being a part of the Madras province of British India, Malabar had its first-ever railway tracks laid in 1862. By the year 1888, trains began to travel between Kozhikode and Koyilandy. It was only three and a half decades later that trains arrived in Kochi. The Ernakulam–Kottayam and Kollam–Kottayam tracks would take another fifteen years to materialize.

Sreedharan continued to stay with his sister's family even after he had finished school in Basel and joined Victoria College in Palakkad. He would visit Karukaputhur on and off. His siblings, who were now scattered across the state and country, would visit the ancestral home in turns.

Sreedharan opted for the science group in Victoria. His subjects were physics, chemistry and mathematics. Seshan too was in his class for the same subject group. Although Sreedharan had joined the college football team, his first love was academics. By now, the direction and shape of his future had been moulded. He had already resolved to finish his studies with flying colours, pursue higher studies and take up a fulfilling career, like his siblings.

Heeding his brothers' advice, he prepared for the engineering entrance test even while studying for his final exams for the intermediate course. Seshan, who had set his eyes on the Indian Administrative Services, had also qualified for admission to engineering. Sreedharan and Seshan secured high rankings in that year's entrance examination. That Seshan's older brother was an IAS officer probably inspired him to follow that path. Many years later, both Sreedharan and Seshan would rise all the way to the peak in their own domains, and even sit together on many committees for central government projects. When Seshan was Cabinet Secretary, Sreedharan was member engineering on the Railway Board. They shared a close friendship, interacting every time they met. They would go extempore in recalling the delightful memories of their long-lasting friendship at the many august platforms they shared. Palakkad's Victoria College had given a reception to Sreedharan recently. The event was attended by his classmates and teachers from his times; many reminisced about Sreedharan as a brilliant academic and a star footballer. It thrilled him no end to visit his classrooms and the campus where he had spent his adolescent years.

Sreedharan joined the civil engineering stream at the Kakinada Government Engineering College in Andhra Pradesh in 1949. The institution has since been renamed Jawaharlal Nehru Technical University. Sreedharan's father would send him money orders at regular intervals. Sreedharan, who stayed in a hostel, would keep most of his money in the bank and withdraw only as much as was absolutely necessary. His thrifty lifestyle maintained his bank account at a steady Rs 100 most of the time. Sreedharan remembers that in his time, the pursuit of a professional degree was not the astronomically costly affair that it is currently. You needed money for fees and books, but even that was nominal. The rest was needed for lodging and food. All of this could cost Rs 45–50 a month.

At the engineering college, Sreedharan diligently pursued his studies, as he always had. Alongside, he developed a great passion for football. He was the college team's captain. Recently, the engineering college felicitated him with an honorary doctorate. The event was also an occasion for the college alumni meet. Many of his college mates attended. The younger generations at the meeting were amused at stories retold by Sreedharan's former classmates recounting his skills in football, in addition to recollections of his academic excellence. But Sreedharan's time with the sport came to an end after he completed his engineering course. Nowadays, he does catch a game on television, especially if the World Cup is under way. But there is no outward expression of the passion any more.

The standard of academics at the Kakinada College was very high. The professors there were renowned for their quality of teaching. Many fellow students of Sreedharan's have reached top positions in various organizations, including the Indian Railways. Although few in number, the engineering colleges at that time were of the standard of the IITs of today. It was possibly due to his training that Sreedharan can instantly recognize the shortcomings of the current Engineering curriculum and methodologies of study. Many a times, he has starkly pointed out the unremitting erosion of values in the engineering industry and in engineering studies and training, as colleges have mushroomed. He openly stated that the loss of standards in professional education, specifically in engineering courses, had already brought great shame to the nation. When he was a student, there were only four engineering colleges in the Madras Province. Now there are so many more colleges, churning out graduates in droves. He wondered how a society could benefit from investments that guarantee no quality!

Every year, engineering colleges in India produce approximately twelve lakh graduates.[2] Yet, the country cannot find enough capable and skilled engineers from among them. The sole reason for this situation is the poor

---

[2] https://fullfact.org/factchecks/india_uk_engineering_science_graduates-29183.

quality of education in these colleges. Sreedharan says we cannot consider an engineering graduate from IIT and another engineering graduate from a random college in Tamil Nadu equally—there is a big difference in the quality of education each has received. There is no attempt to streamline and bring consistency to the education system. There must be a regulatory authority to ensure quality in education. This is not to say that there are not any good private colleges around. But most of them are run as a big business, what with their demands for unbelievable college and capitation fees. What troubles Sreedharan is that some of them happen to be deemed autonomous universities too. You cannot make education just another business, says he. The government must step in to ensure that people from all walks of life have access to higher education.

Sreedharan's apprehensions about the loss of values are not just limited to the subject of training. He observes that the attrition of standards manifests in the abysmal value system in the industry. Even those who have made careers in great organizations are prone to graft. Many of them are in it for the big pay cheque and the superficial titles of the job. Sreedharan criticizes their lack of interest in improving their productivity at work, or in investing in themselves to acquire skills that are relevant and current. He has reiterated his perspectives on training and jobs in the engineering sector on many occasions in his speeches across the country at many prestigious educational institutions. He once addressed a convocation of graduates to say this:

'The opportunity for an engineer to learn never ends until the very end of his life. Every experience will give you more strength. The reward for it will be better and more opportunities to serve your country.

'*Gynameva param balam*—As the saying goes, knowledge is the greatest strength. *Nahi njanena sadrisham pavitramiha vidyate*—ancient wisdom from India says there is nothing bigger than knowledge. If one has gathered knowledge and technical skills, he is equipped with a great inner strength to carry out any task. Your boss or supervisor will respect you as much as you are successful at your work. Your peers will follow and admire you for your accomplishments. This is the lesson I have learnt from the fifty-nine years of my career.

'The engineering industry is a unique one, and offers the highest level of career anyone can aspire for. It commands a role of paramount importance in the world we live in. The growth of any nation depends on how engineering plays its part in it. The engineering sector must be able to uphold the security, health and welfare of the public while ensuring quality in their delivery. Theirs is a community which everyone looks up to as the beacon of values and dutiful righteousness. An engineer will be able to survive temptations to cut corners for temporary and selfish gains. But what I see is nothing but this. There is a great dilution going on in quality and standards now. Corruption is the driving force behind this. Students like you, who are graduating from such esteemed institutions, must hold on to the timeless values like dear life. There used to be a practice in India where students were to give tribute—*guru dakshina*—to their teachers who had imparted knowledge to them. Your tribute to your teachers must be a pledge to stand by professional ethics and your sense of values.

'There is no greatness in achieving the pinnacle in your career if you haven't applied rectitude and quality with integrity when you had the opportunity. I have no doubt in my mind that this is an educational institution of the highest order, but I would ask if there is anything taught here to teach the worth of moral conscience and the value of life. The answer is no. I would like to request the honourable directors to include moral and social values along with the state-of-the-art technical training in their syllabus, to guide these students in their personal and professional lives for long after they are gone from here.'

Sreedharan completed his engineering degree, securing the first rank in his college. Following in the footsteps of his brothers, he too was looking forward to an enriching career to serve society at the highest level he could. He did not think of the Indian Railways at the time, but his brother Krishna Menon urged him to. The Indian Railways offered the highest pay scale among public-sector undertakings. Industry-wise, there was no better place than the railways for a civil engineer to flourish professionally. The professionalism inherited as a legacy of British rule had been ingrained deeply into the 150-year-old institution. Krishna, who was an engineer himself, convinced Sreedharan to apply for a job with the railways, creating a glowing picture of a career there. Sreedharan promptly decided to follow his brother's advice. However, he knew getting into the Indian Railway Service of Engineers was not that easy.

To acquire a career in the Indian Railways Services, the candidate would have to pass the Indian Railways Service of Engineers (IRSE) examination conducted annually by the Union Public Service Commission (UPSC), a test that compares in difficulty with the IAS examination. The maintenance and expansion of the gigantic, nationwide sprawl of the Indian Railways is entrusted to the young and bright engineers selected directly through this process. During the British Raj, these activities were undertaken by military engineers and soldiers. By the end of the nineteenth century, as demands for faster development grew, the British administration deemed it necessary to have a distinct and dedicated department to meet them. Until then, the task of recruitment of civil engineers had been that of the Public Welfare Department (PWD). It was only in 1962 that independent India formalized and brought bills to streamline the selection process for engineers for the railways. The IRSE selects only twenty-five to thirty engineers through the national examination conducted in June every year. The chosen candidates undergo technical training for a period before they are posted on probation as assistant engineer. While in training, they will have to serve in all the divisions of the railways. After their probation, they begin their career as assistant divisional engineers from where, on the basis of their aptitude and skills exhibited on the job, they can rise all the way up to the post of railway board member or even railway board chairman, which is equivalent to the post of ex officio principal secretary to the Government of India.

As soon as he finished college, Sreedharan, keeping his brothers' advice in mind, found a job as a lecturer at the Government Polytechnic in Kozhikode, beginning here a work life that spanned over half a century. He had a particular motive in accepting the job—to prepare well for the IRSE examination to be held in October that year. The polytechnic provided him the ambience and support system for this. Its library had many engineering books that Sreedharan could not possibly afford. Sreedharan made use of everything at the polytechnic to prepare for the IRSE.

As soon as he appeared for the examination, he gave up his job at the polytechnic. Another year was left before the results of the examination would be announced. Sreedharan applied to various institutions for a civil engineer's job. Getting a job was not difficult at all, given his top university grades. He promptly received offers of the post of sub-engineer from both Bombay and Kandla ports. He decided to join the Bombay Port, his decision determined by the fact that his brothers already lived in that city. Sreedharan joined the port in 1953. He did that job for barely a year, although he enjoyed his stint. He was one of the three newest engineering recruits there. His job was at a terminal where oil was transferred from tanker ships that brought it from overseas. The junior engineers were required to train under private contracting companies, and Sreedharan was assigned to train with Royal Engineering Harbour Works, a Dutch contracting company. Sreedharan's proficiencies caught the company's attention in a big way, the result of which was a grant of an increment of Rs 50 every three months. Sreedharan's starting salary had been Rs 350 a month, and by the time he left the port, he was receiving a pay cheque way bigger than what any newbie could ever hope for from his first year at a job. The Dutch firm wanted Sreedharan to continue with them. Sreedharan too had enjoyed port engineering. However, the IRSE results appeared within a year. Sreedharan later credited a part of his success in reconstructing the Pampan Bridge to his short experience in port engineering at Bombay. His early experience in this field must have prompted the shipping ministry to appoint him as head of the shipbuilding yard in Cochin, even without his consent.

Sreedharan secured the seventh rank in the IRSE exam. He did not know that the results had been out until four days after they were released, even though he kept checking the newspapers. During those four days, he was going to the port to work, as was his usual routine. It was a friend who intimated him about the results when he wrote to Sreedharan congratulating him for clearing the IRSE with distinction. The friend too had appeared for the exam. Sreedharan immediately ran back to his house, and scoured the newspapers one more time. His number was there, against the seventh position in the list! The news brought great happiness to his parents and siblings.

The Fledgling Years

Sreedharan was in Kochi, at the location where the bridge across the railway tracks leading into the Ernakulam North railway station was being taken down. The fifty-year-old bridge was about to be decommissioned, to make way for the new transportation system known as the metro to the general public. Jackhammers began to groan, crushing the girders of the old overbridge. As the concrete edifices were becoming a pile of debris, a colleague from DMRC took the liberty to ask Sreedharan, 'Sir, pardon me for asking. I would like to know your thoughts on breaking down a bridge you've built yourself. Does that not make you sad?'

'Not at all,' Sreedharan retorted, with a quick smile. Rather, he said, it brought him happiness of another kind. 'Aren't we building the new bridge and tracks for the metro to serve the demands of a growing city?' he asked. That he was the one to do it again had, in fact, given him all the more reason to feel pleased. The Ernakulam North overbridge was one of the numerous projects Sreedharan undertook when he was appointed divisional engineer (Olavakkode) in 1961.

DMRC had on its list many old and inadequate structures that were to be decommissioned as part of its plan to renovate an ageing city bursting at its seams with a growing population. The old bridges in Kochi were built at the same time when Sreedharan had become a part of the railways that had catapulted the city into a path of rapid expansion and modernization. Sreedharan joined the grand old majestic organization at the time of its golden jubilee celebration in December 1954. He was only twenty-two years old then. His family was elated to see him work for the railways. Although there were engineers from the family, no one had worked for the railways before Sreedharan. Incidentally, no one else from the family has worked with the railways after Sreedharan either. The railways, needless to say, fascinated him; he was fortunate that his supervisors were very well known and had a reputation both for the highest level of industry standards they observed and the impeccable professionalism with which they discharged their duties. Owning a band of the best technologists in the nation, and having a countrywide presence, the railways helped Sreedharan see the world from a much wider perspective. After he had become a permanent employee in the organization, he rose rapidly in the ranks, becoming, within just five years, the youngest divisional engineer in the railways. He successfully led several projects during that period. Along with it came job transfers—four times, and in rapid succession. We will get to those stories in a while.

The Indian Railways was celebrating its 160th anniversary across the country while this book was in the writing. The railways had taken a long time to become the massive and monumental organization it is today. Plans for the first railway tracks in colonial India were laid a decade after coal-powered trains began to run in England. The first-ever passenger train ran between Stockton and Darlington in England. The people who pioneered railway tracks in India were the English traders who turned towards India after having suffered losses from their cotton trade with the United States. They laid a line to the port of Bombay from Thane. The track between Bombay and Thane was almost completed in 1852, and on 16 April 1863, the first-ever train in India rode the 34 kilometres[3] between the two stations. Shortly after that, another train travelled the 38-kilometre track between Howrah and Hooghly in Calcutta. Railway tracks were laid in the south Indian cities of Madras and Bangalore in 1856 and 1864, respectively. In Kerala, the Beypore–Tirur route, which was part of the erstwhile Madras Province, was the first to be laid. That was in 1861. In the same year, the Tirur–Kuttipuram line was also commissioned. It was only after 1888 that the lines were extended to Kozhikode and Olavakkode. Kochi was connected only in 1902. The total length of railway tracks laid in Kerala was about 1673 kilometres as of 2014. However, the grand edifice of the Indian Railways grew immensely to become the largest

---

[3] 21 miles.

railway system in Asia by the year 2013, with more than 14,00,000 employees, and operating more than 20,000 trains a day. The fire-spitting devil—an image sometimes used to scare Indian children into obedience—became the circulatory system of the country, supplying it with life blood for its development.

Sreedharan's first job was that of probation engineer. That designation was accorded to all engineers who joined the railways, by virtue of their performance in the IRSE examination. The first two years would need them to undergo extensive training. They would be typically trained at the Forest Research Institute in Dehradun. IAS officers too received training at the same facility. In fact, Sreedharan met Seshan here, as the latter was part of the IAS batch at Dehradun at the same time. Sreedharan received an appointment letter just twelve months into his training, which was not the norm. The acute shortage of engineering talent in the government services meant that the trainees in that year's batch were posted promptly. Having secured a high rank in the IRSE, Sreedharan was posted in south India, where he had applied from. He was posted in Bangalore initially. He had hardly spent two months there before he had to move to Shoranur in Kerala. Though his stint in his native land did not last very long, he was able to lead many projects that enabled Shoranur to become a major hub for train traffic connecting Kerala and the neighbouring states.

Sreedharan was in Kerala when his father passed away. He was sad that his father would not be around to see him complete his probation and settle down at the job. Neelakantan Moosathu was a gentle but proud patriarch who derived great contentment in watching his children climb up the ladder of glory in their respective careers. He had high hopes for Sreedharan, who had exhibited potential and promise from a very young age.

Construction of the Kottayam–Kollam metre gauge had started during Sreedharan's time in Shoranur. G.P. Warrier, the legendary civil engineer at the railways and a fellow Malayalee, was leading the project. Warrier was a big influence in Sreedharan's professional and personal life. Having closely observed Sreedharan's skills, he invited Sreedharan to work with him. The invitation was an acknowledgement of Sreedharan's competency. Well known as the greatest civil engineer ever in the railways, Warrier's guidance was ever available to Sreedharan, throughout his life on the tracks. It was Warrier who sent Sreedharan out to reconstruct the Pampan Bridge and design the Calcutta Metro as his trusted deputy. Warrier was general manager of the Eastern Railway when he inducted Sreedharan into the team for the Calcutta Metro project. Sreedharan had the good opportunity to work under Warrier in every position—first, as a probation officer reporting to Warrier as his supervising executive engineer, then as assistant engineer when Warrier became deputy chief engineer, and later as executive engineer to Warrier, who had by then become chief engineer.

Sreedharan was appointed as an assistant engineer to build the metre gauge when he moved to the railways' construction wing under Warrier. There were three assistant engineers tasked with completion of the metre gauge between Kottayam and Kollam. Two of them were experienced and reputed engineers, and Sreedharan was considerably junior to them. To be entrusted with the execution of such a complex project under Warrier, and to co-execute it with such an august group of professionals, was in itself an incredible recognition for Sreedharan. While the metre gauge construction was in progress, Warrier got promoted to deputy chief engineer (constructions) and moved to Madras. Sreedharan had spent three years in service while he was in charge of projects in Kottayam. And, unexpectedly, Sreedharan himself got a promotion. However, this also meant that he could not continue on the project to finish the line in Kottayam.

His promotion was something a junior engineer could not possibly have even dreamt of at the time. In October 1958, Sreedharan took charge as the divisional engineer of Baswada division. He was only twenty-six at the time. It was the first time in the history of the railways that someone so young, and with only three years of experience, was thrust into a position that high. (Incidentally, the distinction of being the youngest divisional engineer in the railways would still be his.) This promotion was completely unanticipated. The decision to promote him had been taken as a result of an extensive inspection and review conducted by A.C. Mukherjee, general manager in the railways, in all the divisions across the country. Inspection of any kind would be a routine matter in the railways. Mukherjee's inspections showed that the post of divisional engineer at the Madras–Baswada division lay vacant. Baswada happened to be an important division in the southern region, and had to deal with many problems on account of the absence of a capable divisional engineer. Upon inquiring about the vacancy, the general manager was told by the officers in the division that they could not find a qualified person to fill the post, which Mukherjee, expectedly, would not accept. He asked if there was anyone qualified from the lower ranks for the post. 'There is one; but he is very junior,' they said, hinting at Sreedharan. They also pointed out that the newbie had hardly put in three years at the railways, and that it may not be quite prudent to even consider him for such an important position. 'What's wrong with that?' Mukherjee retorted. 'Isn't he a direct recruit? He must've received appropriate training. Then what are we waiting for? On the contrary, it is imprudent not to give him the job he deserves. Make him the divisional engineer as soon as possible.'

There were two posts of divisional engineer in Baswada—DEN I and DEN II. Sreedharan was given the first designation, which was vested with broader powers than the second. Typically, engineers with over fifteen years of work experience would be considered for these posts. Srinivasa Rao, a senior engineer in the division, was DEN II. Rao, who had been eighteen years with the railways, did not take kindly to someone significantly junior going past him. He shot off a complaint to A.C. Mukherjee, highlighting the issue of seniority. The chief engineer deemed that his claim was legitimate, since Sreedharan was very young at the job. The grievance was but natural. Mukherjee's solution was to swap their positions. DEN II was a position as important as DEN I. Sreedharan took up the DEN II post and continued in the Baswada division for two years, leading several infrastructure development projects.

By this time, S.F. Braganza, who had the reputation of being a firebrand, took over command of Southern Railway as its chief engineer. After assuming the charge, he soon paid a visit to the Olavakkode (currently Palakkad) division for inspection. The division had only been recently set up. The divisional engineer was a very senior Malayalee, P.V. George. Having seen the plight of the new division, Braganza became restless. Not a single project begun under the division was anywhere close to completion. The hospital, workshop, bridges . . . work on all of them had stalled at various stages of implementation. By the end of his inspection, the chief engineer made it clear that the present state could not be allowed to continue any longer. He wanted the present divisional engineer replaced with someone new, he told his private assistant. Chief engineers used to have private assistants in those days. Braganza's PA was a senior officer, Sukumaran. He was asked to name a new divisional engineer for Olavakkode. Sukumaran recommended Sreedharan. Interestingly, Sreedharan did not even know Sukumaran, or Braganza for that matter, in person. Sukumaran wrote in detail to Braganza about Sreedharan, and Braganza promptly reviewed his suggestion and found that the recommendation fit the requirements. Two weeks later, Sreedharan received an appointment letter to join Olavakkode as its divisional engineer.

Southern Railway, even in the fifties, was a vast and important part of the railways. Its footprint was enormous, stretching from Mangalore in the west to Visakhapatnam in the east, and its chief engineer wielded great power and responsibilities. The new division of Olavakkode handled the Podanur–Mangalore line, all the tracks leading to the Cochin Harbour Terminus and the Nilambur line. The division also covered the Jolarpet–Bangalore and Ooty lines. The division was manned by two engineers. Today, this division has seven engineers. A special messenger carrying the appointment letter to join the mission immediately was sent to Sreedharan's home where he was on a ten-day vacation. This was in 1961. More than the recognition it brought him, this opportunity for a second return to his home state made Sreedharan happy. His first posting as assistant engineer in Shoranur had lasted only six months.

As Braganza had wished, the development projects in Olavakkode division picked up pace with the arrival of Sreedharan as its divisional engineer. Within the next two years, every project scheduled for the division—including the establishment's own office building, the railway hospital, living quarters for the employees, drinking water systems, drainage systems, platforms, railway stations and overbridges, were completed. The Ernakulam North overbridge mentioned at the beginning of this chapter was built during this period. Besides the North and South overbridges, the bridge at Shoranur Junction and the overbridge tracks in Trichur (also Thrissur), Palakkad and Kozhikode were built during these years. There was never any problem regarding the funds required for the development projects during that period. Money would pour in if there was intention to accomplish a task. All one had to do was obtain the Railways Board's approval for the plan and estimates for the projects. Unused money from other divisions would be promptly reallocated for the purpose. This practice at the railways helped Sreedharan pick up innumerable projects and complete all of them in the shortest possible time.

On the one hand, the undertakings at Olavakkode division progressed smoothly, but there was trouble brewing from certain corners. The rumbling of the kind of difficulties that Sreedharan would confront in future had already begun to blow his way. As is the case everywhere else, there was a clutch of higher-ranking officers in the railways which was benefiting from underhand deals with private contractors for construction projects. Some of their doings caught Sreedharan's eye.

A senior officer from Tamil Nadu, Komaleeswaran, was the superintendent at Olavakkode division. This post later became that of the divisional manager. He had attempted to compromise the railways to favour certain contractors. Sreedharan put paid to his schemes. The situation went on to fester, with Komaleeswaran consistently attempting shady deals with the contractors and Sreedharan disagreeing with him every time, leading to a cold war between them. Komaleeswaran upped the ante with his tactics, seeking to get rid of Sreedharan from the division for good. Things came to such a pass that it was impossible for the two to get along at all. Yet Sreedharan held his ground, having decided to stay put. The chief engineer, Braganza, had already got wind of the situation, but was not in a position to intervene, although he knew it was spiralling out of control. In such scenarios, if the divisional superintendent and DEN I were to gang up, it was quite easy to put anyone in trouble. Some of Sreedharan's well-wishers in the leadership were worried that he might be trapped in some way. Meanwhile, Komaleeswaran approached the chief engineer with a complaint. Knowing the intent behind Komaleeswaran's machinations, Braganza became livid. After a review of the complaint, he summoned Komaleeswaran to his office and treated him to a tongue-lashing. Braganza vouched for Sreedharan and his commitment to the railways. Realizing Sreedharan's perilous immediate future at Olavakkode, Braganza chose to send a message to Komaleeswaran that if they did not want Sreedharan, he would be more than happy to have him back. But Braganza knew it was not going to get any easier. Reluctantly, he moved Sreedharan to Hubli in 1962, after two years of service in Olavakkode.

To his surprise, Sreedharan found that none other than Komaleeswaran had recently been transferred to Hubli as the new superintendent of the division. Suddenly, troubles began to crop up for Sreedharan again. Komaleeswaran continued where he had left off in Olavakkode. He had

Sreedharan in a complete bind. G.P. Warrier, who had been observing the feud from the time he came to Olavakkode, intervened at this juncture. He advised Sreedharan that time and life were too precious to waste entangling oneself in inane ego trips. At that time, Warrier was chief engineer in the construction department. He asked Sreedharan to join him. Sreedharan too felt that that would be the right choice for him. Under Warrier, there were surveys being done to convert the Londa–Margao line to broad gauge. Sreedharan took up the post of executive engineer to lead the effort, while also assisting in other assorted projects. For a while, he had worked with the Hassan–Bangalore construction crew as well. Warrier's mentoring moulded the engineer in Sreedharan significantly. Warrier, reputed as the premier technician of railway civil engineering in the nation, recognized the spark in Sreedharan, and made sure the genius would fulfil his tryst with destiny.

Pampan, the First Signature

The pillars of the Pampan Bridge, ravaged by a cyclone, were reinstalled while the sea was still in the mood for another round of devastation. But after Sreedharan was done with the reinstallation, no engineer had to ever go back to the bridge to redo it. So many cyclones have since rolled past the bridge and so many storms buffeted it, slamming through the Palk Strait as they headed for Kandy and Talaimannar in Sri Lanka.

It was as though Sreedharan could hear the heartbeats of the islanders of Rameswaram—cut off as they were from the mainland—the way he proceeded to rebuild the bridge, finishing it in half the allocated time. The country was overwhelmed with pride and gratitude for the thirty-one-year-old, who was but a divisional engineer in the railways; indeed, the world took notice of the young engineer from Kerala who had repaired the longest sea bridge in India.

Sreedharan had moved from Olavakkode to Hubli, from where he went to the central office of constructions for Southern Railway in Bangalore before he joined the mission to rebuild the Pampan Bridge. Sreedharan got married when he was at the Olavakkode division, almost at the end of his stint there. The wedding was held on 21 October 1961. Radha, the bride, was the daughter of Dr Achutha Menon, a very well-known doctor from Ponnani. Sreedharan's brother Karunakaran too got married the same day. His wife, Parvathy, was Radha's older sister. Their weddings were solemnized one after the other, their timings scheduled in keeping with the traditional calendar drawn up for auspicious events. Karunakaran tied the knot at the Thrikkavu Temple in Ponnani. Sreedharan's wedding ceremony followed, at the bride's home. Sreedharan being busy at work, his brother Krishna Menon took care of all the wedding plans and arrangements. Sreedharan did not even meet Radha until after they got betrothed. Radha was in her second year of study for a bachelor's degree. After the nuptials, the newly-weds began to live in the railways colony in Olavakkode.

The feud with Komaleeswaran that had begun much earlier boiled over now and culminated in Sreedharan's transfer to Hubli. This happened soon after his marriage. Sreedharan took Radha along with him. It was just the first of their countless moves from one city or town to another. 'After we got married, Radha has always been with me, except during her pregnancies, when she would go to her mother's. Other than those times, we would all go wherever my job took us. The tradition still goes on,' Sreedharan says. In another two years' time, Sreedharan found himself having to go to Bangalore, as Komaleeswaran's harassment had become insufferable. The post was technical private secretary to the chief engineer of railways constructions, P. Krishna Raju. It was during this period that Sreedharan was assigned the mission of reconstructing the Pampan Bridge. His job as private secretary lasted only eight months.

On 23 December 1964, there was shocking news from the southern tip of the nation. The cyclone had sent waves that rose so high that they licked the Pampan Bridge clean at night. The skyscraper waves were only a few in number. However, the second wave that rose about 30–40 metres high at around 11.30 p.m. washed away the bridge in one sweep. Unfortunately, precisely at that time, train number 653, the Pampan–Dhanushkodi passenger, was on the bridge. Nobody on that train could be saved. Except for the engine, the sea had swallowed up all the other parts of the train. The coaches, made of wood, crumbled like flimsy toys and vanished in the waters. The storms and floods that ensued wiped out the city of Dhanushkodi. Its port, schools, places of worship, its countless business establishments, thousands of homes and, above all, its human population . . . everything was gone. With the bridge washed away, the tragedy snapped the only connection the islanders had with the mainland. The 2345-metre bridge, which had lasted a century, had lost 125 of its 146 girders to the sea. Two of its concrete pillars were gone too. The Sherzer Bridge, which had a rolling lift to let ships pass through the channel, had been damaged too.

The Indian Railways' immediate decision after the tragedy was not to reconstruct the bridge; it did not seem a dire necessity, Rameswaram having already lost its earlier glory and the prominence it once had as a trade centre. The railway tracks that had been destroyed ran across Rameswaram to the east end of Dhanushkodi. The island of Rameswaram was close to the eastern shore of the state of Tamil Nadu, and extended southwards into Sri Lanka's Gulf of Mannar. Dhanushkodi was the southern tip of the island, with the Bay of Bengal on the east and the Indian Ocean to the south. The distance from Rameswaram to Dhanushkodi was hardly 18 kilometres. What prompted the British to lay a track from the mainland to Pampan, and then onwards to Dhanushkodi, was the proximity of the latter to Sri Lanka, which was only 16 kilometres away from the land's end. The bridge was built in 1914. The centenary celebration of the bridge in 2014 included elaborate programmes, including wide-ranging technical seminars. After the railway bridge was built, another bridge had come into existence to facilitate road transport to the island. This miracle, conjured up by British engineering talent, stood the test of time and held the distinction of being the longest bridge across a sea in India until at least 2009, when the 5.6-kilometre Banda–Worli Sea Link was commissioned.

Earlier, the train tracks had been laid only up to Mandapam. The Dhanushkodi extension was done later. You could buy a single passenger ticket to get from India to Colombo in Sri Lanka. The train would take you up to

Dhanushkodi, from where one would have to hop on to a ship to Talaimannar and from there board another train to reach Colombo. Modern times saw the introduction of many other modes of travel, which reduced the pre-eminence of Pampan in later years. Rameswaram, and therefore Dhanushkodi, had considerably lost their attraction as a destination for traders.

However, the railways' decision not to rebuild the bridge became a major point of contention. It was the only lifeline that connected the island with the mainland. More than that, Members of Parliament (MPs) from north India had a special interest in Rameswaram, it being a spiritual destination for Hindus. At any rate, the north Indian political lobby's attention to the matter came as a relief to the people of the island. Tamil Nadu had not grown as a powerhouse of politics yet. The initial decision not to rebuild the bridge had to be scrapped. The revised plan was to build the bridge only up to Rameswaram. The earlier bridge split into two at Pampan, one arm leading to Rameswaram, the other to Dhanushkodi. The Dhanushkodi portion would be left out in the new plan. Nobody opposed it.

When tragedy struck Pampan, Sreedharan was at Karukaputhur on a Christmas vacation from Bangalore. Soon, there were calls for Sreedharan to report back at his office immediately. Cancelling the vacation, Sreedharan returned to Bangalore, where the chief engineer explained the emergency call. He briefed him on the Pampan tragedy and instructed him to go to Madras as soon as he could.

Sreedharan immediately took off to Madras and met the deputy chief engineer, who explained the railways' new plan to him. The broken bridge to Rameswaram would have to be rebuilt within six months, and it would be Sreedharan's responsibility. It was, undeniably, a daunting task. But the decision had come straight from the ministry of railways at the centre. Sreedharan had to head straight to Rameswaram at once, said the deputy chief engineer, finishing his brief. It was only much later that Sreedharan came to know it was G.P. Warrier who had suggested his name for the job. Warrier did this because the minister's office demanded that the mission be completed as fast as anyone could possibly do it. Warrier let his superior officers know that there was a brilliant engineer who could accomplish the mission just the way they wanted. The phone calls were made to Sreedharan in Karukaputhur right after their parleys. In the end, after he had rebuilt the engineering marvel wrought by the British, the world had come to know about Sreedharan, the gifted engineer. Destiny had swept him into its arms, marking out Sreedharan for the world of fame and recognition.

The deputy chief engineer handed over the railways' plan for the reconstruction of the bridge, as well as other technical documents, to Sreedharan. The 126 girders that had been washed away had to be rebuilt, including the one that was partially damaged. The new ones would be made and brought from distant locations such as Gujarat and Assam, where the facilities for building them were located. Support would be provided to Sreedharan's team to haul the barges and cranes to the bridge. However, there was not even a minute to lose. The deputy chief engineer demanded that the job must be done within six months, and not a day more. Sreedharan paid attention to the minutest details, collecting all the information he could before heading out to the site, but did not make any promises to his supervisor. If it were to be done the way it had been described to him, the mission was not going to be done in six months. Moreover, the condition of the bridge could be assessed only after someone had actually visited the place. Everything else had been mere conjecture. How could one give his word on the basis of speculation without a ascertaining the reality at ground zero? This was how Sreedharan approached the situation. Meanwhile, something unexpected happened. As Sreedharan left the Madras office, the deputy chief suggested that he meet the general manager as well. B.C. Ganguly, general manager of Southern Railways, was one of the best civil engineers in the Indian Railways' hall of fame. Sreedharan dropped by Ganguly's office. Having inquired about Sreedharan's task, Ganguly broke the news that even the six-month deadline which he had agreed to earlier was not really acceptable now. At best, he could give Sreedharan three months to get the bridge functioning again. Sreedharan, who had the utmost respect for Ganguly, heard him out. He could not bring himself to say no to someone whom he revered as a guru. He let him know that he was on his way to Rameswaram to ascertain the facts on the ground, and set off straight for Pampan.

After his arrival in Pampan, Sreedharan spent the first two days surveying the area and the broken bridge to assess the situation. Having seen the tragedy of Pampan up close, Sreedharan realized what a dire state the bridge was in. The century-old bridge had been completely destroyed. Let alone the new three-month deadline, the initial estimate of six months by the deputy engineer itself appeared impossible. There was no way out. Though the girders could be ordered and built at many different facilities at the same time, six months would not suffice for their transport. The country's infrastructure was still rudimentary compared with the improved systems it possesses today. The only means to move supplies and materials to the site had already bitten the dust and was now washed off into the sea. Sreedharan scrambled for alternative solutions, while ideas and instructions came thick and fast from the administration. Sreedharan knew none of that was going to make much of a difference. But he did not give up hope.

Meanwhile, Sreedharan had gleaned some news from the local fishermen, which brought him a ray of hope. While fishing in the sea, they found many of the washed-away girders submerged not too far from the coastline. The fisherfolk pointed out to him a few locations where the girders were lying undersea. This was only a happenstance, but Sreedharan could not pass up the tiniest sliver of opportunity that presented itself; in any case, he did not have any other means by which he could finish the mission his superior officers had entrusted to him. He went on an

expedition with the fishermen to find the lost girders. He
went wherever the local fishermen led him. Many girders
lay on the sea floor, a couple of kilometres away from the
Pampan Bridge, at a depth of 40 to 50 feet under the sea.
The water was crystal clear; if you looked long enough, the
girders could be seen from above the surface of the water.
None of them were damaged. If Sreedharan could recover
those steel girders, he could solve the problem easily. The
fishermen were overjoyed to learn that their scouting could
be of huge benefit to the railways. They began to scour the
sea vigorously, and upon striking new finds, brought news
of them to Sreedharan instantly.

Having come this far, Sreedharan realized that it
was possible to finish the reconstruction earlier than he
had thought. This was the time to begin the core leg of
the mission, which Sreedharan termed a 'triumph of
engineering ingenuity'. The goal was to work around the
girder specifications, tweaking the available resources to
accommodate them while also conforming to the required
industrial equations. The next step was to chart an extensive
plan of action to utilize any and all resources to get the job
done. Sreedharan's early experience as a port engineer in
Bombay now came to his rescue. He had already learnt
about the behaviour of the sea during low and high tides.
This knowledge helped him overcome the challenges of
operating in a marine environment.

Work now picked up a brisk pace. A crane had been
brought to Rameswaram at the beginning of the mission,
but that was not enough. One more was brought in so that

the girders resurrected from the sea could be bolted to the pillars from either side of the bridge. Sreedharan designed and built the crane for this purpose, not wanting to spend precious time on finding one and getting it transported over. The next task was to build a barge sturdy enough to support the conduits to pull the girders out of the water. Sreedharan designed that too, and sent the order for its execution to the workshop at Arakkonam. He had a friend at the workshop, P.M. Joseph, who was of great help in getting it done expeditiously. Sreedharan had asked him to make one for him in 48 hours! The job was finished to a tee, and the barge was brought to Rameswaram by a special train. A boat tugged the barge to the locations where the girders lay. Local fishermen dove deep into the sea with giant iron hooks to attach to the girders, which would then be pulled slowly out of the sea floor with a winch. A ramp of rails was made, to haul the girders over the bridge. After the girders were cleaned and freshly painted, a system, to 'pitch and place' the girders between the pillars, was developed. As soon as the girders were placed across the pillars and bolted, the rail tracks were laid on top of the bridge right away. New rail tracks had already been brought to the site earlier.

Sreedharan employed workers from the famed community of Mappila Khalasis, who were known for their traditional and highly effective methods of hauling massive objects, especially ships. They did their work to perfection. However, even if one girder were to be erected each day, four months would pass before all of them could be done, easily spilling beyond Ganguly's aggressive deadline of three months. Sreedharan's motley crew took about a week to install the first girder. However, as the mission evolved, the Mappila workers began to show their mettle in the specialized area they had come to assist in. Their work picked up a speed that in no time progressed in leaps and bounds. If the first girder took them a week, the second took four days, and the third, three days. With the available resources and the techniques perfected over a couple of weeks, it became a smooth task to rapidly put all the girders in place. Towards the end, the workers had begun to haul two to three girders a day on to the bridge.

As soon as a girder was raised, rails were readied to be bolted on to it. A crane would run on the brand new rails to the far end and begin installation of the next segment of girder and rails. All this was accomplished with the help of machinery designed and developed during the course of the reconstruction, for the sole purpose of meeting the unique needs and circumstances of the project. Each of the 126 girders consumed by the sea was recovered and restored to bring about the rebirth of a broken bridge. Not one of them suffered damages in the process.

Metro-bound

There was an amusing side note to the incredible story of Sreedharan's resurrection of the Pampan Bridge when the Union minister for railways and the government embarrassed themselves, as they were caught unawares by the early completion of the mission. The minister for railways S.K. Patil made an incorrect statement on the status of the project's progress, not knowing that the last girder was being hoisted the very same day. The minister, responding to a query in Parliament, claimed that the Pampan project was progressing quickly and would take another month to complete. That he said so without checking the facts on the ground left both him and the government red-faced. The time allocated at the beginning was three months, and only a month and a half had passed since the mission began. Naturally, and given the scale of the mission, the minister did not think twice about making the statement that it would take at least another month. But what happened that night was quite the opposite. The last girder raised from the sea had been bolted to the pillars and the rails laid on top. Sreedharan and his band of workers unfurled the green flag for the first post-cyclone train to pass across the bridge. What remained were 44 days to the deadline that Sreedharan's wisdom had saved.

That night, Akashvani announced news of the installation of the last girder of the Pampan Bridge, mentioning the successful trial ride of the train too. The authorities, who had not been keeping abreast of the progress of the Pampan mission, had irresponsibly passed on a wrong status update to the ministry. The next day, the print media took over the news and celebrated it, much to the chagrin of the ministry and the government. They immediately demanded to know the root cause of the confusion, in an attempt to spare themselves further embarrassment. Truth be told, most of the superior officers did not quite have enough of a grasp on Sreedharan's engineering exploits and technical skills to be able to brief the government adequately. They had not paid attention to the details, beyond reading the routine site reports on the progress of the project. However, the feat fetched wide appreciation. The minister for railways himself declared a cash award of Rs 1000 for Sreedharan, for having completed the project earlier than the estimated time. That was the first-ever recognition Sreedharan received for excelling at his job. Soon there would be a long line of awards, including the Padma Shri and the Padma Bhushan, coming his way.

It would be hard to imagine the Pampan effort would have been pulled off had someone else been in charge in

Sreedharan's place. Many government engineers would most likely have followed the time-tested bureaucratic modus operandi of pen-pushing—ordering the new girders, waiting for them forever, and taking an additional seven or eight months after their eventual arrival to complete the project. Had such an officer been told by the fishermen about the girders lying under the sea, he would have typically ignored the opportunity rather than thinking out of the box to recover them. Sreedharan's ingenuity and commitment saved the railways not just time, but real money estimated to be in crores of rupees. And to think that there were only two assistant engineers reporting to Sreedharan. It was at this time that his daughter was born, whom he didn't go to meet until the task was accomplished.

Sreedharan and his assistants lived in Rameswaram for the entire duration of the project, lodged in a crummy railways guesthouse. The storms had not just damaged the Pampan Bridge, but had also flattened Rameswaram and Dhanushkodi. All the infrastructure was gone, and Rameswaram had become a ghost town reduced to a pile of rubble. The high tides and the deserted coast, without any trace of human life, created an eerie atmosphere there. The island was condemned to temporary isolation, except for the occasional emergency calls that were made to the mainland. Although Sreedharan did not face trouble on the scale he did on the Konkan project, the short mission of Pampan was strewn with its own unique challenges.

After completing the bridge, an anemometer was installed on it to monitor wind speed and direction. The device would alert inhabitants if the wind speed exceeded 55 kilometres per hour. Giant tsunami waves were to test the bridge again in 2004. However, this time the storm that had crushed Dhanushkodi and reduced it to a haunted hamlet half a century ago headed to Talaimannar instead. Recently, a ship collided against the bridge, causing minor damage to one of the pillars.

Reminders of the wild wind that slammed Pampan in 1964 still abound in Rameswaram and Dhanushkodi. A monument dedicated to the memory of the dark days, when thousands of lives and a whole township perished in the tragedy, stands at Dhanushkodi. The world took notice of Sreedharan after the Pampan mission, and the media sang paeans of praise to his leadership and resourcefulness.

After this mission, Sreedharan went back to Bangalore to continue his work as technical private secretary to Chief Engineer P. Krishna Raju. He participated in many important track development projects in the southern region. Soon, another promotion came his way; he now became a deputy chief engineer. However, Southern Railway had no vacancies to accommodate him in this position. The process of seniority-based promotion was determined at the federal level, which did not consider whether positions were available to accommodate the promotees. Such a position was available only in Calcutta. Sreedharan's policy of accepting job transfers without protest meant that he would be ready to move to Calcutta, although he was not excited about it. As usual, he travelled with family in tow. One convenience about the railways was that transportation of furniture and other household paraphernalia was a smooth affair when it came to job transfers. The railways' workers would always be there to box one's belongings, which would be hauled across the country by rail wagon; and the railways' properties in the form of quarters were available everywhere for the transferred families to occupy right away. Sreedharan, therefore, never really worried too much about the pains of job transfers—at least, not until his children grew up. Afterwards, his constant transfers hindered the smooth progress of education for them. Sometimes, they had to switch schools more than once in the same academic year. By the time Sreedharan took up his new responsibility in Calcutta, G.P. Warrier too had joined Eastern Railway as general manager. The surveys and planning for the long-awaited Calcutta Metro project had already been underway for a few years. The decision to build the modern transportation system was taken at the highest level under the railways' watch.

It had been hardly three months since Sreedharan moved to Kolkata and had his children join a new school—the oldest went to high school, and the younger ones were in the lower grades—when he received a message to relocate to Bilaspur. This time, Sreedharan left his family behind, going to Bilaspur by himself. For the first time, his transfer made Sreedharan a little uneasy. One day, G.P. Warrier called him to his office. He knew about Sreedharan's reluctance to move to Calcutta in the first place, and understood that his sudden transfer to

Bilaspur and the isolation from his family troubled him a lot. Warrier inquired about his current job. He asked if Sreedharan would mind continuing with Eastern Railway. Sreedharan responded sincerely in the negative. Warrier again asked if Sreedharan might not like an opportunity of a different kind. In the end, Sreedharan agreed to Warrier's suggestion to join the Calcutta Metro. This was the period when the Calcutta Metro was hiring capable, young engineers. Earlier on the same day that Warrier spoke with Sreedharan, the metro's chief administrative officer had visited Warrier, who had instructed him to have Sreedharan on the team. Warrier had not even proposed the offer to Sreedharan for his opinion!

Sreedharan joined the Calcutta Metro in 1971. He spent five years in the city. Those five years were valuable learning time, and would eventually set him on the path that saw him earn the sobriquet of 'Metro Man'—the person who brought state-of-the-art metro transportation systems to India. His position in the metro project was deputy chief engineer (planning and design). The post carried quite an attraction in terms of the challenges it posed, since the country had never had a modern metro system until then. It called for the envisioning, design and construction of tunnels and metro stations that would run their entire course of 16.45 kilometres underground.

Calcutta was building what would be the fifth metro in all of Asia. It would be pertinent to digress a bit and describe the state of metro transportation in other countries, and the importance of metro systems to modern city life in general. There were many distinct factors that distinguished the metro—also known as rapid transit, underground subway, elevated railways, metro, metropolitan railways, etc.—from other, traditional modes of public transport systems to move large numbers of passengers from point to point in the fastest way possible. The metro had become hugely popular as the choice mode of transportation for modern civilization, its security and efficiency being its top features. The metro needed the least amount of land and other geographical resources for its construction and upkeep, while it could carry the maximum number of commuters. The pollution it generated was significantly low. Although its maintenance was a costly affair compared with traditional transportation systems, the metro's overall benefits far outweighed the expenses.

The Tube in London celebrated 150 years in 2013, by which time more than 188 countries around the world had metro systems, and another fifty countries were building new ones in their cities. Asian countries, which are the latest entrants to the metro world, embraced the metro to such a point that they have left the European countries far behind. Japan built its Tokyo Metro—the first in Asia—in 1927. Osaka got the next one, in 1933. Today, Japan has the fastest-growing metro systems and, naturally, leads the world in metro technology. The metro chains in Tokyo have grown and crisscrossed the city to such an extent that commuters in Tokyo would half-jokingly say they could never be sure where they would go at any given moment. In other words, Japan's metro networks have such reach that they now provide the highest level of accessibility to people from every corner of the country. Japan supports many metro projects commissioned in India, with either finance or technology.

China too has a rapidly growing network of metros. The first was commissioned in Beijing, in 1969. Every year, China builds more than 150 kilometres of metro lines. India acquired the capability to build 25 kilometres of metro rail only after the Delhi Metro was built. The communist country of North Korea built a metro in 1968–69. Pyongyang Metro, which has two lines laid entirely along 22 kilometres of tunnel, is the 'deepest' rail line in the world, running 110 metres below the ground. It broke Kazakhstan's record of a metro built 105 metres underground. North Korea treats its metro somewhat as a hideout from the warfront, since the country sees itself at perpetual war with its enemies. South Korea too had built a metro by 1970. The affluent Gulf countries adapted to Metro systems rather late. Dubai had a metro system only in 2009, while Saudi Arabia's metro in Mecca opened in 2011.

The Calcutta Metro took long years of planning (for perspective, the oldest metro in the world was built just ten years after the Indian Railways was established). The authorities thought up the idea as a solution to the chaotic inefficiencies of the city's transportation system, its burgeoning population and soaring pollution levels. The deliberations as to how to build a metro had begun as early as 1949. A detailed metropolitan transport project was drawn up in 1969, and the central government approved the plan in 1971. Working on the metro plan, Sreedharan very soon realized that although the world had gone quite far with advanced technologies, even the technical experts of considerable repute within the Indian Railways hardly had any real knowledge of the system. Everything had to begin from zero. There did not even exist the knowhow for building metro platforms, let alone the trains. But Calcutta could not wait for very long.

Meanwhile, an international conference on metro systems was being held in Japan. India too had an invite. The railways considered this timely and beneficial, in view of the metro project being planned in Calcutta, and decided to send J.M. Roy, the metro's chief engineer, to the event. The Railway Board itself asked him to go to Japan. He was to learn everything he could in order to build the Calcutta Metro. Surprisingly, the chief engineer himself declined the offer, and wrote back to the Board saying he had only a couple of years left in service and that the investment of time and effort on him would not be prudent. There were plenty of young and capable engineers working for the metro project and, in the long-term interest of the railways, one of them ought to go, he said. He recommended Sreedharan as his replacement. Roy's action amazed Sreedharan. Nobody in those days would let go of any chance of a foreign trip. The railways did indeed have worthy leaders like J.M. Roy who thought and acted selflessly, keeping the larger cause in mind. The turn of events overwhelmed Sreedharan, but pleasantly so.

The week-long conference was an eye-opener for Sreedharan. He picked up a lot of knowledge about the technologies that went into the building of a metro. He was not going to be content with just that. It was important to see the wonder of the Tokyo Metro up close, and possibly talk to the technical experts. He would stay on in Tokyo for four more days after the conference got over. He could not expect the railways to finance his overstay in Tokyo though. What then could he do? He found a solution. He contacted a relative in the USA and requested some money. The relative promptly sent him enough money to enable Sreedharan to stay an additional four days in Japan. He got in touch with the Indian embassy in Tokyo and let them know his plans, requesting their support.

Sreedharan was in for a warm surprise at the reception given to him by the embassy. The embassy officers got to know about his time of arrival from the conference venue. When he landed in Japan, the officers were respectfully waiting with a vehicle for him at the airport. They had already made arrangements for his four extra days of stay. Sreedharan shared his programme with them. He needed to visit the Tokyo Metro and, if possible, meet the engineers at the design office. The embassy officers got into action right away to schedule the visits and meetings. Sreedharan took the greatest advantage of his stay in Tokyo. He let himself loose on the metro, and had long discussions with the technologists at the design centre. He also picked up ideas for model designs from his conversations with them. That was the beginning of Sreedharan's enduring relationship with Japan.

The Shipyard's Captain

The four days spent in Tokyo helped Sreedharan lay the foundation for the design of the Calcutta Metro. Given that even a basic understanding of metro technology had not taken root in India, the world flung open to Sreedharan in Japan appeared vast and extraordinary. Having seen, experienced and been convinced of the quality of the Japanese metro technology and systems, he returned home carrying a few designs for the Tokyo Metro in his bag. Unfortunately, the descriptions on the designs were in Japanese, a language of which Sreedharan had no knowledge. But the brilliant technocrat possessed the language of an engineer, and managed to decipher the sketches and designs with some effort. As he gleaned details from what, to him, was like reading hieroglyphics, he was able to hone a prototype for the Calcutta Metro. Sreedharan fondly recalled that the priceless treasure of designs he brought from Japan are still stored carefully at the metro office in Kolkata.

On 29 December 1972, after the designs were ready and the preparatory work for their implementation had been carried out, Prime Minister Indira Gandhi laid the foundation for the project. Five lines totalling 97.5 kilometres were advised as part of the project. The first phase consisted of three lines; they were the Dum Dum–Mahanayak Uttam Kumar, Bidhan Nagar–Howrah Maidan and Dakshineswar–Thakurpukur lines. The initial excitement was not sustained for very long. In fact, the project itself was in danger of losing steam. There was no progress of any sort for almost three years since the prime minister had laid its foundation. It had become a comatose victim of the old bureaucratic malaise of dawdling incompetence. Various elements, who should never have been associated with a project of the prominence of a modern metro, held back its progress. There was no coordination with the state government on the project, which was an undertaking of the railways. Things got to a point where there was no more money coming in. The project had to rely entirely on the annual railway budget to subsist, and this nominal allocation served only to keep it alive. The drying finances meant that it could not procure land for construction; even the land that had been acquired had not been paid for, and the contractors began to desert the project in droves.

Sreedharan realized that the project was heading down a path unfamiliar to him. He was terribly demoralized. His heart too was no longer in the project. The cost of construction skyrocketed at the rate of lakhs of rupees a day. After five years of its launch, the project's first phase was nowhere near completion. It took eleven years for the first phase of the 9-kilometre Esplanade–Bhavanipur line to be completed. The entire project took another eleven years! By then, the technology employed to build the metro had become awfully outdated. In summary, as the world and time had mercilessly moved on, the metro in Calcutta was bogged down by a mindset of a forgotten period.

Sreedharan says of the metro experiment that it was a relegation of the technology of the modern world to the background, and a dumbing down of it to an Indian administration's version. The planning phase itself got derailed. None of the trains or signalling systems were the best in their class; rather, they were of the lowest quality. And not because the best was not available, but because there was a spoke in the wheel created by some old-timers of the administration who had proved to be irrationally defiant when it came to the choice of indigenous products and technology. The railways' decision to handle this project was patently ill-advised. It could not be the railways' responsibility to build urban infrastructure for mass transit systems. The railways too arrived at the same conclusion, but only after it was too late. After twenty-two years, and at a cost fourteen times the original estimate, the metro in Calcutta huffed and puffed to the finish line in 1995. In terms of real money, the Indian Railways had spent Rs 1600 crore, against the original estimate of Rs 140 crore. Despite metro systems being the top choice for passenger transportation around the world, the disastrous experience of constructing the metro in Calcutta, paradoxically, emboldened the opponents of the system in India. The legacy of failure and stigma associated with the metro lingered, until the grand success of Delhi Metro became an important chapter in the history of mass transportation in India. When Sreedharan was at the helm at DMRC, a plan was formulated to renovate the metro system in Calcutta (by now renamed Kolkata), but the railways showed no interest at all. The plan targeted investments from the private sector to finance the project. The railways had to invest only 35 per cent of the entire budget. Even that did not excite the railways into action, making for another disappointment in the series of unfortunate events faced by the Calcutta Metro.

A sense of oppression had overcome Sreedharan by the end of his fourth year with the metro in Calcutta. He was convinced of the futility of continuing there. Meanwhile, he received another promotion in 1976, to the position of divisional superintendent. The posting was in Mysore. 'Don't go to Mysore. Stay back in Calcutta,' the general manager had insisted. The Railway Board too was of the same opinion. But nothing would sway Sreedharan. He wanted to go, and he stood his ground. Thus did Sreedharan leave the Calcutta Metro, a dream-turned-nightmare. He took charge in Mysore and stayed there for two years, until promotion to the post of additional chief engineer took him to the headquarters of Southern Railway. The subsequent posting, as chief engineer (constructions) in Eastern Railway, brought him right back to Calcutta. Until then, Sreedharan had been accepting all the transfers in his stride, considering the expansive reach of the colossal organization of which he was but a cog. But now there was a new problem—the education of his children. Sreedharan and his wife personally never worried too much about job transfers. But they realized that it was affecting their children, who were now stepping into higher education at different levels. The constant change of schools, as well as the new languages they had to learn every time they moved to a different state, made studies difficult for them. Their parents had to do something about this. So they decided to have all four of them join the Kendriya Vidyalaya. These central schools were functioning everywhere in the country; their standard of instruction was considered very high, and they would guarantee an atmosphere of continuity for the children. Upon their second coming to Kolkata, all of them joined the Kendriya Vidyalaya. Sreedharan could continue in Calcutta for only another six months. In the meantime, a significant responsibility came up in the form of a deputation.

Sreedharan was sent to Cochin as chairman and managing director (CMD) of Cochin Shipyard. The assignment came to him quite accidentally. There was no replacement for Vice Admiral Krishnan when he retired as the shipyard's CMD. Instead, the decision was to find someone from prominent portfolios to fill the post. The construction of the first-ever ship from the Cochin Shipyard—*Rani Padmini*—had already been begun. The objective was to find a competent head for the institution, so that the project would be completed on schedule. The union ministry for shipping expressed its intent to bring

someone on deputation to pre-empt the appointment of
a newcomer whose inexperience could potentially delay
the project. Interestingly, Sreedharan had no inkling about
this. He did not even apply for the position.

The shipping ministry sent out circulars to all other
ministry offices to recommend capable personnel to fill the
post of CMD for Cochin Shipyard. The railways responded
to the request by suggesting Sreedharan's name without
his knowledge. They must have considered his impeccable
professional record, the shipyard's specific needs and the
first-hand experience he had had at Bombay, even though
it was for a short period. Shortly, a cable message arrived in
Calcutta asking Sreedharan to report at Delhi immediately.
There Sreedharan met the general manager, who asked
him to appear for an interview for the post of CMD for
Cochin Shipyard. A surprised Sreedharan told him that he
hadn't applied for it. But the general manager insisted he
attend the interview nevertheless.

Sreedharan had no reservations. Although it would
mean he would not be working with the railways, here
was an opportunity to get out of Calcutta and head to
Kerala. But the railways was loath to part with him;
many there wanted him to stay with the organization.
That much was made clearly evident in the words of the
general manager. Bidding farewell to Sreedharan, he said,
'My wish is to have you here with us. I would prefer not
to lose you after the interview. But if you go, I bet they
are going to choose you.' The general manager's hunch
became a reality.

The one year Sreedharan spent with Cochin Shipyard was replete with adventure and upheaval. The destiny of the shipyard, a central government institution, was about to be rewritten over a period of just thirteen months, during which the organization sailed past unimaginable milestones. The first one was, of course, the manufacture and commissioning of its first-ever ship, *Rani Padmini*. This set the shipyard on a pedestal in front of a proud nation. It was during this mission that, for the first time, Sreedharan had to deal face-to-face with the force of organized trade unions. And perhaps that was the only time too. Apart from that aspect, the practice of foreign procurements, behind which lay an unholy nexus of bureaucrats and political masters siphoning off thousands of crores of rupees, was dealt a mortal blow before Sreedharan had finished with his historic mission at the shipyard.

When Sreedharan took charge, the shipyard, which had been established in 1969 and was now a decade old, was in an abysmal state. It had been considered a key component of the nation's infrastructure development strategy, but had shown no evidence of any prominent standing, either in its work culture or its output. On the one hand, there was the CMD and his sycophant officers, and on the other, the united and potent might of the lower-ranking employees and the labour force, standing defiantly as their detractors. Both sides picked frequent fights on sundry issues. With Sreedharan's coming, everything now moved by the book. He had walked into the shipyard as it was reaching new lows, where the values and culture behoving a centralized, strategic organization such as a shop to build ships were coming apart alarmingly.

As usual, Sreedharan arrived in Kochi with his family. All four of his children joined the Kendriya Vidyalaya in Willingdon Island. He got the Shipyard House that was assigned as the CMD's residence. He was the last CMD to live in the Shipyard House. None of his successors were willing to overlook the limited conveniences the house offered. Till the end of his time at the shipyard, Sreedharan lived in that house.

Sreedharan's first task as CMD was to bring about an acceptable level of professional discipline and respect for schedules and commitments among the officers and the workers. At the railways, these were routine practice. The most important requirement for this was to follow a strict policy of timekeeping for all employees, including high-ranking officers. The goal was to make sure that everyone was reporting to work and discharging their duties on time. Until then, it used to be a free-for-all, where everyone, top officers included, would come and go as they pleased. The high-ranking officers would habitually sign in, indicating that they had reported for duty, and soon leave their stations to run their own personal errands. Sreedharan personally caught a few who would thus sign in and vanish regularly from office to attend to their private matters, sometimes even to build their private houses. He dealt with them with an iron hand. Anyone who reported to work after a certain time was booked for tardiness and instructed to take half a day off. At any rate, the brisk actions brought about a sea change in the organization. A majority of the employees adapted to the new style of functioning, while a section remained intractably resistant. Though Sreedharan never paid attention to the offenders, he bore their unforgiving wrath at times. But their antics could not scare him in any way. He never shied away from threatening punitive action to quell insolence and insubordination. Sreedharan remembered he never had to actually carry out any of the threats, as the handing out of charge sheets itself yielded the results intended.

The second in the line of reforms he brought in at the shipyard was an interactive forum to communicate with the workers every Monday. It was called Open Monday, aka Somwar Durbar, held from 10 a.m. to 12 p.m., during which time anyone with a complaint or suggestion could approach the CMD directly. Open Monday was a significant step in the process of overhauling the work culture at the shipyard. However, a section of the workers vehemently opposed it. Sreedharan realized the need for such a forum as soon as he began to interact closely with the workers. He had a morning routine of taking a stroll around the company's hulls on the way to his office. His paid regular visits to the hulls every day at 8 a.m., dressed in white shorts, T-shirt and shoes. This routine prompted the workers to show up early. Gradually, Sreedharan showed an inclination to listen to them and receive their complaints. He learnt that in their capacity as workers, they had their own suggestions and concerns for redress.

He came up with the idea of scheduling a day and time for such activities on a regular basis. That was how the Open Monday programme came into existence. Every Monday, Sreedharan would receive a huge pile of notes from the employees and labourers. He would find solutions to the issues described to him in writing even before the session started. He would listen to, and try to resolve, every issue brought to him during the session. In the case of more complex problems, he would involve the complainants in reviewing and checking facts to arrive at a resolution, with their participation in the process. For the employees, the very fact that someone was listening to their everyday issues infused them with confidence and boosted their morale.

However, the workers' union at the time did not take to Open Monday too kindly. They detested the CMD's practice of accepting complaints directly from workers, which was akin to subverting the core concept of an organized trade union. The leadership of the union asserted that only they could act as a mediator on behalf of the workers. The prominent trade union, the Shipyard Employees' Union, had a president, S.C.S. Menon, who was a powerful trade union leader and a general secretary, Thampan Thomas, who had been an MP too. The union demanded that Open Monday be shut down right away. Sreedharan defiantly rejected the demand. He made it clear that, as head of the organization, he reserved the right to receive complaints from employees, and that they should be able to meet him at any time they wished to. The union, never on board with Sreedharan's reforms, was itching to set the stage for a protracted battle. However, not everyone in the union thought alike, Sreedharan recalled. S.C.S. Menon and Thampan Thomas were reasonable leaders, willing to see his perspective in the larger interest of the organization. But there were a few bad apples with special interests in the union, whom Sreedharan could not bring himself to submit to.

Thampan Thomas expressed agreement with Sreedharan's view of the situation much later, when he recalled Sreedharan's time at the shipyard. Until then, the CMD and the management in general used to take the labourers for granted. Their basic rights and needs were routinely denied. One could not be sure if the CMD was even aware of this. The institution was run abysmally by the middle-level officers, who were incapable of discharging such duties. They were happy to take punitive measures against workers in the lower grades, whom they would blame for any losses resulting from their own ineptitude and lack of foresight. The workers, having been subjected to such rotten treatment, viewed Sreedharan's actions with distrust, Thampan Thomas said. There were several pressure groups in the union. Some of them got together to dub Sreedharan an enemy of the workers. On the contrary, Sreedharan never showed any interest or dislike for any political ideology or leader, observed A.J. Antony, the production manager who had worked with Sreedharan. Sreedharan's thrust was to create a healthy environment for the workers to do their best, and the only way to make that happen was to address their concerns. Sreedharan would always say that behind every problem, there was an element of discontent of some sort. The challenge was to be able to figure that out and find a solution, rather than yield to mindless pressure and threats. Antony vouched for Sreedharan's convictions as he watched him act on them firmly and steadily. Unfortunately, the workers' state of mind at that stage would not allow them to see the big picture. The section in the union opposing Sreedharan mulishly stuck to their agenda of seeing him gone. However, their collective might was not strong enough to make Sreedharan beat the retreat, as proved in the events that were to follow soon.

Man of Unflappable Steel

As the duel between Sreedharan and the union played out, he had to engage in yet another joust in parallel. This was related to his appointment under the shipping ministry as a CMD on deputation from the railways. Sreedharan joined the shipyard while he was a chief engineer in the Indian Railways. The rank of CMD was higher than that of a chief engineer in the railways. During the interview, Sreedharan was promised the salary of a CMD, which the Ministry reneged on as soon as he assumed the position. They let him know that their intent was to give him a salary commensurate with his position as a chief engineer of the railways. The broken promise and the attempts to justify his lower salary on the basis of a posting made by way of deputation had irked Sreedharan.

He wrote to the shipping ministry several times expressing his disappointment. The ministry stood their ground. Ultimately, Sreedharan decided that if he was not going to get the appropriate grade for the job he was doing, he would not continue any more. He let them know his decision in writing. The ministry did not relent. In the original contract, Sreedharan was to occupy the post for five years. However, the ministry reserved the right to terminate the on-deputation job any time after the first year. Sreedharan sought to use that clause to get himself out of the shipyard. The shipping ministry wished to have him continue there, given the state of the shipyard at that time. These exchanges continued until Sreedharan chose to push the envelope beyond a point, forcing their hand.

Ignoring the daily din of trade unions protesting reforms and the pressure from the shipping ministry on the issue of his pay grade, Sreedharan focused on his core objective of fast-tracking the efforts to float the organization's first-ever ship *Rani Padmini* into the waters. It was not going to be an easy task to schedule its completion, given the crawling pace of the build. Sreedharan's arrival had significantly sped up its progress. The initial responses to his actions as CMD had given him a lot of confidence and encouragement, leading him to believe that the build could be done on a schedule. Sreedharan announced a date when *Rani Padmini* was to be floated—26 January 1980. The workers' schedules were adjusted, and they were given additional responsibilities to accomplish the goal. However, the trade union that had declared an open war with Sreedharan used the occasion to their advantage. They began a policy of 'Go Slow' as they stubbornly stuck to their opinions and demands. All the higher-rank officers had agreed to work three shifts a day. They were willing to work overtime for the cause. But the union chose their position vindictively, declaring that none of their member-employees would work a third shift. Sreedharan was not going to yield to their will. He exhorted the officers to do the job the workers would not do. Rolling up their sleeves, they took to the dock. A great majority of the workers were actually pleased with the new culture that was driven by a clarity of purpose, and liked the style of functioning that was emerging for the first time at the Shipyard. They rallied behind Sreedharan in complete faith as he led them from the front. Meanwhile, there were a few incidents that vitiated the environment at the workplace.

The shipbuilding had been progressing according to Sreedharan's plan. One day, a group of workers mobbed and physically harmed their supervisor. It was a reaction to his decision to report to work, defying the union's diktat. Sreedharan suspended the perpetrators of the violence immediately. Now, the union came to the fore and declared a complete strike at the shipyard. They decided to snub even the call for talks, demanding that the CMD withdraw the suspensions. But Sreedharan made it clear that the aggressors had to come clean. His unyielding position on the issue was now spoiling the union's plans, but they would not relent either. The strike continued without an end in sight, as the feuding parties stuck to their guns. It was time for the state government to intervene and defuse the situation. Chief Minister E.K. Nayanar called up Sreedharan to discuss options for a way out of the deadlock. Sreedharan explained his side of the issue and reiterated that he would not step back an inch from his original decision. 'This is not like the railways. If the issues aren't sorted out the right way, the shipyard would have to be locked out. Nobody shall lose anything except these workers,' was Sreedharan's unambiguous response. The government too realized that the standoff had gotten worse. The time for the management and the workers to talk to each other had already passed. Realizing the dire need of the hour, Nayanar invited both the management and the union leadership to Trivandrum, the state capital, for talks. The CMD decided to bring himself to Trivandrum to represent the management. The union brought their leaders, including S.C.S. Menon.

The meeting started at dawn and went on for the whole day. With the fractious arguments that dragged on and on, it appeared that the meeting was stumbling headlong into a stalemate. The main sticking point was Sreedharan's inflexible stand on the issue of the workers' suspension. The union had already retracted most of their demands. In fact, they were ready to call off the strike, but wanted the suspension of the workers involved in the attack to be revoked. Sreedharan was not ready for that. He would not change his decision, but simply reiterated his position on the disciplinary action. This provoked the union leaders so much that one of them, in a fit of rage, swore at Sreedharan, threatened him and stomped out of the meeting room. Seeing how the meeting was getting out of control, the chief minister took Sreedharan aside for a private conversation. This standoff must end, he said. It cannot be allowed to go on any longer than it already had. The only demand the union had now was to lift the suspension of four workers. Sreedharan had to cooperate this one time, he suggested. Should these workers be involved in another incident of violence, Sreedharan would be free to terminate their employment, and no questions would be asked. The government would not interfere. But currently, it was time for a compromise, without which he could see no end to the situation. Sreedharan agreed to Nayanar's appeal. When both groups had come to an agreement and left Trivandrum, it was already 3 a.m. the next day.

Although none of the above incidents hampered progress on *Rani Padmini*, the ship could not be built by the scheduled date. Work shot two weeks past the scheduled date of 26 January. The ship was eventually brought to water on 9 February, amid much gaiety and fanfare. Sreedharan followed what would mark all future celebrations of completed missions headed by him. Only a few, unavoidable invitations were sent to personalities from the political and administrative leadership. He made sure that people from various sections of the society were adequately represented. The people of Kerala, and particularly the residents of the city of Cochin, had shown a special interest in the development of the shipyard from the very beginning. This was evident, since they had done their part in the struggle to continue the legacy of the shipyard. The media too displayed great interest in the goings-on at this unique institution. *Rani Padmini* being the first-ever ship built at the yard, its commissioning

attracted quite a bit of national attention. The large ship
was the first of its class to have been built in the country.
Sreedharan expressed his desire to have one of the employees
lead the ceremony of guiding the ship into the water. But
the officers and workers disagreed. They pointed out that
floating a ship into the water was an age-old ritual and
insisted that the tradition of getting a woman to do it had
to be honoured appropriately, as it is anywhere else in the
shipping world. He was told not to bother calling anyone
else; the ritual would have to be done by his wife, they
said. The recommendation was made, and the vociferous
cheering that followed, egging on Sreedharan to accede,
finally had its effect. He agreed that his wife Radha would
help *Rani Padmini* to be brought to the water from the
shipyard to the Kochi Lake, and into annals of history.
Radha broke a coconut that day to signal the start of the
celebration.

Some of the central ministers who had expected to
be invited, as a matter of convention, had been excluded
from the inauguration, much to their chagrin. This
fanned the embers of discontent in the shipping ministry
with Sreedharan. If you analyse Sreedharan's modus
operandi at various stages of his projects—the Konkan
Railway or the Delhi Metro, where he had independent
authority or oversight—you would know this, that upon
reaching a major milestone in the project, he would never
celebrate it in the company of political heavyweights or
random ministers. Only once did he have a minister at
such a function, and that was former minister for railways

George Fernandes. It was at the very beginning of the Konkan Railway project. That never became a precedent, as it never happened again. However, there were instances when representatives of the people sought out the special events and showed up themselves. The prime minister had inaugurated the Delhi Metro project in an understated ceremony in which even the Delhi chief minister had no real role. Many had misgivings about being left out during these occasions, but they adapted to Sreedharan's general approach towards celebrating success.

Meanwhile, Sreedharan's disagreement with the shipping ministry on the question of pay grade had grown into a confrontation with them as he entered the next phase of his mission at the shipyard. This time, the sticking point was the plan to buy engines from abroad to build three more ships, following the success of *Rani Padmini*. It was then that the powers that be decided to get rid of Sreedharan. Until his time, the ships built in the country had been using German-made Mann engines. Poland too made engines in the Shultzer class that matched the German brand for efficiency. But the shipyards in India had always bought the German brand, even when the Polish alternative was only half as expensive. Buying German-made engines was a traditional practice for India, and no shipyard authority had the courage to question the practice, since the actors behind these deals where none other than the top officials of the shipping ministry and other political hotshots in the central government. Typically, each shipyard would give its engine requirements to the shipping ministry which, in turn, would deliver the engines without allowing the shipyard authorities to be part of the procurement process.

Cochin Shipyard needed not one, but three engines, and the transaction was going to be a multi-crore-rupee deal. Having been convinced of the efficiency and the competitive price of the engines from Poland, Sreedharan approached them with the order. His decision to overlook Mann engines shook the power structure, sending shivers down their spine. Sreedharan tried his best to make them see reason, but could not overcome their resistance. They would not have engines from anyone but Mann. Sreedharan listed the technical and financial benefits, illustrating them with side-by-side comparison charts to convince them, but to no avail. In the end, disregarding the opposition he faced, Sreedharan decided to go it alone. The stage was set for a battle.

Meanwhile, the board of directors of Cochin Shipyard sat to discuss the plan. They evaluated the technical excellence of the Polish engines and, concluding that Sreedharan's views were right, declared their unanimous support to him. There were frenzied, closed-door meetings and counter-tactics being hatched in Delhi at the same time. The shipping ministry declared that the board's decision would be overturned and the order would go to Mann. Sreedharan would not surrender. He made it clear that the board's decision was paramount. The controversy soon boiled over into the media, who presented the story endorsing Sreedharan's position on the deal. The trade union that once had no love lost for Sreedharan changed its opinion on him now; the workers were full of admiration for his stand and threw their support behind him. Eventually, the shipping ministry and the minister himself had to submit to the mounting pressure from several directions. The tradition of purchasing Mann engines had suddenly come under the spotlight, and rumours of backroom deals diverting tax money in lieu of commissions flared up in public debates, much to the discomfort of the ministry and the government. The incident brought Sreedharan a groundswell of support among the common people and his own workers. It would be worthwhile to note that since then, Cochin Shipyard has always procured Polish engines for the ships they built.

The episode extinguished any benevolence the shipping ministry had towards Sreedharan and their wish to see him continue as CMD in Cochin. They brought out Sreedharan's earlier letter to them, in which he had expressed his displeasure over his pay grade. The ministry used this letter against him, citing his unwillingness to work at a lower pay grade—paradoxically, just as he was going about his job with great panache and even greater popular support. He had shot off that letter to the ministry within the first three months at the job. To have him at the helm at that time was their need, and they ignored his request. But now that he had turned the tables on them, they were itching for a ruse to give him a quick send-off. The ministry was in possession of his letter of discontent, which it could interpret to describe his removal from the post as a voluntary withdrawal by him. The ministry brandished the letter at him as it elbowed him out of the shipyard. The real reasons for his ouster remained a mystery to the public. Sreedharan knew what was brewing in the backrooms of the ministry early enough, but he chose not to go back on his original decision to step away.

When the trade unions heard that his deputation had been cut short, they demanded in one voice that Sreedharan not be removed from the post. A letter signed by the workers and union leaders was sent to the shipping ministry, which conveniently ignored it, having made up its mind. The subsequent events would justify Sreedharan's reforms at the institution, although appreciation of his work came a bit late when his former foes rallied around to prove him right. In the beginning, the union had attacked many of his actions vehemently, but there was no doubting that his policies were squarely intended to further the institution's growth. P.K. Kunju, a trade union activist and a welder during Sreedharan's time at the shipyard, could recall that they viewed Sreedharan as a conscientious technocrat. Kunju was an assistant manager at the shipyard in 2012 when he was interviewed for this book. Only after Sreedharan was gone, after a year of groundbreaking events, did the workers and employees realize the value of his leadership. He had not approved all of their demands. He made sure his authority was unimpeachable in his own inimitable way. The mighty, organized trade unions of the day and age were not going to back away under strong-willed authoritarians. But they realized that apart from the initial animosity they felt at his style of functioning, no unsavoury incident of any kind had happened at the shipyard. Until Sreedharan's time, there had been several ugly clashes at the Shipyard, including an agitation by workers at the gate of the CMD's private home. A coterie of high-ranking officers used to run the shop. Sreedharan had them sidelined unceremoniously. He could not be swayed by bribes or servile sycophants. He was utterly fearless as he repeatedly made provocative decisions and breezily went about the business of implementing them. Kunju recalled how Chief Minister E.K. Nayanar, who would habitually impose his will on career officers, showed great restraint and fondness for Sreedharan during the entire duration of the marathon negotiation with the trade union.

The shipping ministry had their way, even in the face of tremendous pressure from all fronts. The ministry had made up its mind not to have Sreedharan a minute longer. This unilaterally put an end to Sreedharan's mission at the shipyard, which had lasted just a year. Although he was working at a lower pay grade and was denied the benefits commensurate with the job, Sreedharan wanted to continue as CMD, having done all the hard work to set the stage for bigger goals for the shipyard. He had become happy with the general atmosphere at the shipyard, which had shown a gradual turnaround, the workers showing greater acceptance and appreciation of his leadership. Thampan Thomas remembered Sreedharan's emotional farewell speech to the workers.

Sreedharan headed many institutions, working with all kinds of officers and workers for fifty-seven years, during which he rarely had to come face-to-face with organized unions. What stood out in each of his encounters with them was his unmistakable acknowledgement of their relevance and significance. One could argue critically that he did not like the way the trade unions traditionally functioned. This was probably because Sreedharan's studied and novel approaches required greater appreciation of the big picture he had in mind while going about his missions. This was the reason why the shipyard's trade unions were initially at war with him, but also the reason that they later turned around and pledged their unequivocal support to him. Earlier, the reforms Sreedharan had brought to the shop floor to improve work culture and productivity were summarily rejected, and the unions made it a goal for themselves to see him fail miserably. Soon, they learnt the real scope of the intent and vision behind Sreedharan's actions, and rallied around him at a critical juncture, demanding his continuance at the shipyard.

The next time Sreedharan came across a trade union, he was CMD of the Konkan Railway. There too while agreeing to their reasonable demands, he dauntlessly countered their practices and policies that were detrimental to the institution. In the beginning, the Konkan mission had no trade union. But, influenced by the powerful unions in the railways, the Konkan Railway workers began to organize themselves soon. There was tremendous pressure on the management to get the unions approved. Eventually, the

Konkan workers' union flourished quite well, although Sreedharan would never allow the workers to indulge in union activities at the expense of their duties and responsibilities. He took prompt and strong actions against anyone guilty of negligence or indiscipline, regardless of his or her status in the hierarchy of the union. This had caused some friction in the beginning, but soon afterwards, Sreedharan never had to have another confrontation with trade unions anywhere else.

Later in life, when plots were being hatched to expel Sreedharan from the Kochi Metro project, a section of the media had unearthed the old stories from his time at the shipyard from the archives. It was not a coincidence that his second coming to Kochi after three decades brought him opposition similar to that his first stint had. Both assignments bear testimony to his unflinching conviction and belief in the professional and personal values he cherished and never compromised. The eerie similarities, unfortunately, proved that crooks in the bureaucracy and government had endured, driven by greed and malice, with their preconceived agenda to counter conscientious officers like Sreedharan. The same people who had earlier feigned great joy at Sreedharan's leadership of the Kochi Metro changed colour and tried to repel him, fretting that their bluff might be called. To discerning observers, this looked like a sordid rerun of the many ignominious episodes from the past. The media echoed their sentiment, and accused the scheming group of behaving like fly-by-night operators in trying to oust Sreedharan so that they would not be inhibited in extracting commissions through shady deals for the purchase of foreign equipment. Luckily, history did not repeat itself entirely. There was a surge of popular demand for Sreedharan to lead the metro project, and a parallel demand that the key responsibilities of handling tenders had to vest with DMRC. There were demonstrations, including human chains snaking 25 kilometres along the proposed metro line. As the entire society rallied behind Sreedharan with one voice, the plotters had to back down without inviting any more attention to themselves.

Stepping Down from the Railways

Having returned to the railways from Cochin Shipyard, Sreedharan did something he had never done in the twenty-five years of his professional life. Now promoted as chief engineer (constructions), he put in a request to be assigned to Southern Railway and be given a post in Madras. That was the first and last time he had approached his supervisors with any kind of request. Until then, his policy was to go wherever he was asked to go. He never complained about the many inconveniences he had to endure personally. Radha and the children had gotten used to them too. But now that his kids were in the higher grades at school, the need to settle down in Madras was driven by his desire to provide a good education to them. It took a lot out of him to drop the request to Kishan Chandra, who was the member engineering on the Railway Board. Sreedharan met him personally when Chandra came to Ernakulam for the inauguration of the Ernakulam–Trivandrum broad gauge line to make his appeal. Although Sreedharan no longer worked for the shipyard, he had continued to live in Ernakulam. Chandra ruthlessly rejected his request. He snapped at Sreedharan, saying he would not entertain requests for preferred posts; and that instead, Sreedharan must be ready to work anywhere he would get posted. That was how it was done in the railways, Chandra had said.

No doubt Chandra's response disappointed Sreedharan, but not for long. Soon, there was an unanticipated development. Prime Minister Indira Gandhi disbanded the entire Railway Board, unhappy with its functioning. This was something that had never happened, before or after, in the history of the Indian Railways. Her action startled the organization. Another board was assembled almost immediately. Neelakanta Sarma, who was from Kerala, became the member engineering on the new board. He was from Ambalapuzha in Kerala, and knew Sreedharan very well. Sreedharan called him up and let him know his circumstances, explaining that he had not been posted anywhere since his stint at the shipyard. He would prefer Madras for his next posting. Much to Sreedharan's relief, Sarma told him he was going to sign such an order, which would have to wait for the minister's signature, and meanwhile, Sreedharan could head to Madras right away. The order would arrive by the time he reached Madras. Everything happened exactly the way Sarma had promised. He took special care to get the order dispatched to Madras within just two days. Sreedharan was appointed as chief engineer (constructions) in Madras.

Then followed a period during which Sreedharan could work uninterruptedly in one place for the longest time he ever had. He worked in Madras for five years, until 1986, in his new capacity. During this time, he undertook numerous construction projects for Southern Railway. All the major lines were doubled. Quite quickly, the divisions in Southern Railway went on an overdrive as scores of projects were embarked upon. They included the construction of the Tirunelveli–Nagercoil track, the doubling of the Podanur–Ernakulam line, the construction of the Karur–Dindigul line, the building of the Moor Market and the tripling of the Madras–Villivakkam–Avadi lines. This was also the time when the design and construction of the suburban railway in Chennai for mass transit began.

Sreedharan's mother passed away in 1983, when he was in Chennai. Her sudden departure hit him hard. One day, he received a call from his brother Krishna Menon saying his mother was not doing very well, and that Sreedharan should visit Karukaputhur as soon as he could! Sreedharan did not wait. He handed over responsibilities and, making other arrangements to prepare for his absence at Madras, hopped on to the earliest homebound train. He arrived at Karukaputhur by midnight. His mother's condition was not encouraging. She had had a stroke and one half of her body was paralysed. Sreedharan spent that night at the hospital. The next day, the siblings moved her to a nursing home in Trichur to provide her better medical and hospice care. His mother remained in the nursing home for a month. Sreedharan spent the whole time at her bedside, tending to her needs. The only time he went out of the hospital was to visit his brother's house in town in Trichur to wash up. Upon his arrival at his mother's bedside, he had already called the general manager's office in Madras to let them know that he would need a long time off. His mother lived another month before she passed away. She was ninety-two. Her death deeply affected Sreedharan. One could not be more grateful for her sacrifices and the great care with which she nurtured her children, said Sreedharan. She made sure the children grew up to be empathetic and generous, instilling in them universal human values even as they were forging ahead in their careers. The values she had passed on to them were the family heritage, to cherish for generations to come. They were so well integrated in her children that they not only followed them, but proved more than worthy of passing them on to their own children. When it came to his mother, Sreedharan would abandon his usual measured manner of speaking and become effusive; no words were enough to describe how his mother, although innocent of letters, was able to impart to her children a balanced perspective on life.

In 1986, Sreedharan was promoted to the post of chief administration officer (CAO). His posting was in Bombay. He was not in the least interested in moving out of Madras at that point, since he had only five more years left for a graceful retirement from the railways. He was so reluctant to move out of Madras that he rejected the promotion. R.K. Jain, a well-known administrator, was chairman of the Railway Board. Sreedharan telephoned him about his decision. The chairman was taken aback. Jain explained that the position of CAO was a very important one. 'You shouldn't turn it down. You still have a long way to go. This is the pedestal from which you launch yourself as a general manager or member engineering on the Railway Board. Please accept the promotion and join immediately in Bombay for my sake,' he remembers Jain telling him. His earnest request got Sreedharan reconsidering his decision. You would not expect a senior to convince you the way Jain did, he thought to himself. He realized the chairman had expectations from his assumption of the new post. One should not dismiss such a request. He changed his decision, leaving for Bombay to take over the responsibility.

The problem of relocating the family again came up. They could not come along right away. The children's annual exams were underway. He could not find an alternative home for them for the short period they would remain in Madras. Kumar Das, a traffic officer who was being transferred from Bombay to Madras, suggested a way out. Sreedharan's quarters in Madras had been allotted to him. Das could stay with his sister's family nearby until Sreedharan's children were done with their exams. An immensely grateful Sreedharan could now keep his family comfortably in Madras as he headed to Bombay. There he worked as CAO for eight months, during which he also had to take care of the general manager's responsibilities for Central Railway. That post had not been filled for months. Vijay Singh, who was to take over the position, had sustained a fracture in an accident, forcing him to go on an extended leave of absence. This meant that Sreedharan had to do two jobs at the same time.

In 1987, Sreedharan was promoted as the railways' general manager. This opened to him the opportunity to become the powerful member engineering on the Railway Board. But there was another general manager who was senior to Sreedharan, Eastern Railway's Gouri Sankar. Although they were both of the same age, and had been batchmates too, Gouri Sankar had the seniority, which for the railways has traditionally been the principle criterion for postings and promotions. Hence, it was clearly Gouri Sankar's turn to become member engineering on the board. However, there was a different climax to the story. It came about quite unexpectedly. The railway minister at the time, Madhav Rao Scindia was not inclined to let Gouri Sankar become member engineering. In reality, there was no friction between Gouri Sankar and the minister, but the financial commissioner was the agent provocateur. He had shot off a highly damaging note on Gouri Sankar to the ministry. With that, the doors of opportunity were, unfortunately for Gouri Sankar, closed to him. The ministry was forced to consider the next eligible candidate, which was Sreedharan.

The Railway Board is the highest body in the Indian Railways, set up to facilitate technical and policy-related activities to develop the organization. A place on the board is the peak of achievement for anyone starting off as an engineer in the organization. Sreedharan remained member engineering on the board until the last day of his thirty-six-year career in the railways, when he retired in June 1990. M.N. Prasad, another Malayalee, had been Chairman of the Railway Board. The only Malayalee to reach this position before him was G.P. Warrier. The board used to have five members. It has now been expanded to include two more. Sreedharan retired before his turn for consideration for the post of chairman came. However, ever dynamic, he made good of his position as member engineering very well. It was during this time that serious discussions to revive the Konkan Railway project were warming up.

Having spent a long career in the railways, and having been in the mainstream of the enterprise, Sreedharan has always had the greatest respect for the giant institution. He calls the organization a 'huge family'. 'You tend to get the feeling of being part of the family, regardless of what division you were in,' he would say. It was a statement that easily resonated with every individual associated with the railways. You get to work with talented professionals as colleagues in all corners. Sreedharan would never tire of pointing out that the railways have had the least incidents of corruption among government organizations, even as it has continued to be the largest employer in the country.

Another reason for his admiration and gratitude for the railways was the steadfast support and encouragement he continually received from the big names in the organization. B.C. Ganguly and G.P. Warrier were two of them. Besides those two mentors, there was a long line of exceptional professionals along the way. Sreedharan had learnt a lot from each of those worthy colleagues. Their lesson to him lay not just in the sheer dedication they showed to their profession, but also in their thoroughbred bearing as models worthy of emulation, in the way they balanced their official and personal lives with transparency, purity of intent and integrity of the highest order. They were all wizards who had constructed miracles for the railways. G.P. Warrier was one such personality. His genius lay not only in the legacy of engineering he left at the railways, but in the path he pioneered, and his methods that became models to be followed for project management in the public sector. Warrier recognized Sreedharan's brilliance in delivering construction projects very early. On his part, Sreedharan found a role model and a guru in Warrier. Sreedharan's brother Padmanabha Menon was Warrier's batchmate at engineering college. That could be one of the reasons why Warrier played mentor to Sreedharan. Ever since Warrier took Sreedharan under his wing to build the Kottayam–Kollam metre gauge, he always included him in all the major construction projects of the railways. M.N. Prasad says the opportunities and encouragement bestowed upon Sreedharan by Warrier played a significant role in shaping Sreedharan's future accomplishments. The most important lesson he taught was to adopt an uncompromising attitude towards completing every task efficiently and on time, while also assuring transparency of the highest order. Naturally, Warrier was a taskmaster. He recruited workers after scrutinizing their skills and personality threadbare. There was no question of compromising on quality and efficiency. At the same time, anyone in his team could approach him for anything. He was the model Sreedharan followed during his stint at DMRC.

Warrier had contributed enormously to the development of the railways throughout the country, especially in the all-important gauge conversion of the entire rail network across the nation. You could get a glimpse of his foresight and genius from the simple fact that he had accurately predicted the future of the railway systems and kept in mind developments in the future when he implemented the metre gauge, decades before anyone else thought of it. The Kollam–Ernakulam metre gauge line runs over several bridges. When the metre gauge lines were replaced with broad gauge ones, the only major component of the track that had to be removed was the girders. He had constructed the bridges several decades ago, and in such a way that they were sturdy and durable enough to accommodate future developments. Prime Minister Indira Gandhi inaugurated the first broad gauge in a ceremony where the Union deputy minister for railways, Mohammed Shaffi Qureshi, lauded Warrier's foresight that saved the nation time and money.

Warrier's career in the railways flourished steadily until he became the Railway Board chairman, a post he held from 1975 to 1977. After retirement from the railways, he became Bharat Heavy Electricals' CMD. He was also chairman of Rail India Technical and Economic Service (RITES) and IRCON; CMD of Kerala Minerals and Metals and a member of the Planning Commission. He retired from active work to spend the rest of his life with his family at his home in Madras. Sreedharan believed Warrier was never given the recognition he deserved, considering his immense contributions to the railways. Warrier wrote a book on his times at the Indian Railways, titled *Time and Tide: My Railway Days*. But this book too vanished, in the same way Warrier's place in the history of the Indian Railways had. Not even a single copy of the book can be found anywhere today.

Later in Sreedharan's career, the role of B.C. Ganguly in moulding his personality, and the uncommon wisdom he imparted to his protégé in the field of project management, could never be overemphasized. Ganguly was an extraordinary technocrat, and a project manager who had played a pivotal role in adopting and accelerating modernity in the railways. He used to be known as the 'super professional' for his efficiency. He too had been chairman of the Railway Board, during 1970–71. Unfortunately, he was dismissed from that position and from the railways, making for a sordid chapter in the organization's history. Ganguly had joined the service in 1937 and served for thirty-four years, during which he was instrumental in building a solid foundation for the railways to embrace modernity. His ill-fated spat with the then minister for railways Hanumanthaiah culminated in his unceremonious ouster from the board. Differences over what constituted development for the railways led to a war of ugly, personal one-upmanship between Ganguly, the seasoned technocrat, and the minister backed by the

Congress party. Once, while on an official journey by train from Delhi to Rajasthan, the minister's henchmen blocked Ganguly in his salon and heckled him. Following the minister's orders, Ganguly's salon was detached from the train a few minutes before it started on its journey. Sufficiently provoked, Ganguly instructed that the salon be locked down where it was left. Having seen him respond to the political arm twisters in kind, the Congress party decided to get rid of him. Ignoring his stature and his unforgettable contributions to the enterprise, and with scant courtesy towards the genius of an engineer who had given a lifetime to the railways, he was ruthlessly booted out on 10 October 1971. After the incident, Ganguly led an obscure life, his spirit irreparably broken. He passed away in Calcutta in 1986, at the age of seventy-two.

Sreedharan never shied away from passing on the same love and affection he received from his predecessors in the railways to the young and able greenhorns who flourished under his watch. He took care to bring in brilliant professionals from the Indian Railways to the Konkan Railway or even to the Delhi Metro project, which had remarkably different needs compared with the railways, in terms of technology and administration. There were many young engineers who had been with Sreedharan since the time of the Konkan Railway and, until recently, with the metro project in Kochi. Sreedharan had been directly involved in handpicking the band of professionals who would work on his construction projects, following the rules and regulations he set for each of the missions.

Sreedharan's style of functioning never compromised on the composition and culture of his team.

By the time Sreedharan retired in 1990, he had worked in almost all the divisions of the railways. He had worked in the capacities of executive engineer, divisional engineer and deputy chief engineer in the south and south-eastern divisions. His story of twenty-five job transfers in a span of fifteen years had been the focal point of some debates on him. That someone of the stature and eminence of Sreedharan had been subjected to frequent and mindless job transfers had been criticized in the media. Sreedharan's response was typically understated when he explained that that was how the railways has always operated. The railways needed their band of highly skilled personnel to spread themselves around to acquire maximum exposure and gain greater skills. There was nothing suspicious about the practice, he said.

Following his retirement from the railways, plans for larger and more complex responsibilities lay in store for him. The Konkan Railway would be the greatest and most adventurous leap in infrastructure development—an amalgam of technical knowhow fired by a daredevil imagination—that post-independent India was going to witness. More than the courage of the authorities in setting out on this daunting adventure, what was lauded and valued was the decision to hand over the mission's control to Sreedharan.

Konkan: An Epic

We are at Ratnagiri railway station, one of the major stations along the Konkan Railway line. Erected at the entrance of this station is a structure rather unusual for a railway station. It is a memorial for the martyrs who lost their lives during the formidable exercise of laying this line. Each year on 14 October, wreaths are laid in front of this structure, the Shram Shakti Memorial, to mark the organization's gratitude to those workers. In the cool morning of October, when you feel the first stirrings of yet another winter, you will observe a two-minute silence if you happen to be at any office or station on the 760-kilometre Konkan line that runs through 59 stations spanning three states. The Konkan Railway is headquartered in Navi Mumbai, in a building called Belapur Bhavan, and has regional offices in Ratnagiri in Maharashtra, and Karwar in Karnataka. The trials and tribulations of the Konkan mission had been witnessed by the nation for seven years, from 1990 onwards, and there used to be all-round dismay every time deaths were reported from the construction

sites. An enormous number of workers had died along
the treacherous terrain. The Konkan line, with the sea
on one side and the green hills on the other, had come
at a staggering cost. The memorial is a tribute from the
organization to the contributions of everyday people to the
building of a nation.

Bisecting the Western Ghats across the states of
Karnataka, Maharashtra and Goa, what Indian workers
built under Sreedharan's leadership was indeed an
engineering marvel hitherto not seen in the country. It
had no precedent. The engineering protocol and project
management methods were innovative. For this reason,
the scripts for all large-scale projects in the country that
followed contain a few lines of indebtedness to the Konkan
mission. It was not just the largest infrastructure project
undertaken and delivered in post-independent India until
that time; it became the very blueprint for all large schemes
of infrastructure development. The railway line of 760
kilometres had 92 tunnels along the way, out of which
at least nine were more than 3 kilometres long, and the
longest approximately 6.5 kilometres. Consider the longest
tunnel ever made in India until the Konkan mission—the
2.2 kilometre tunnel that ran under the Lonavala Ghat
on the Mumbai–Pune route. The Konkan project also
had 149 large bridges and 1819 medium-to-lower-sized
bridges. Over 21 kilometres of those bridges crossed water
bodies from end to end, while 300 ran over or under
roads. The 2.2-kilometre bridge built across the Sharavati
River near Honavar was the longest. The tallest viaduct

in the country also belonged to the Konkan Railway; it was erected between Nandi and Panvel near Ratnagiri. Its pillars were 64 metres high, shorter than the Qutub Minar by only 4 metres. That it took only seven years and three months to accomplish this gigantic mission in a country like India added extra sheen to its success.

It is a mechanical task to reel off the numbers and list the milestones achieved by the project, but a near-impossible one to record in words the gargantuan effort that all this entailed. Four states—Maharashtra, Goa, Karnataka and Kerala—participated in the project. This alone constituted the first set of hurdles, as the contrasting and sometimes conflicting political environments in these states made it difficult to get them all to agree on anything, leave alone an experiment of the size of the Konkan mission. Another challenge was the treacherous terrain of the route, with its swamps, rapids, rivers and jungles. The stretches that ran through easier, inhabited terrain raised other difficulties, such as those relating to land acquisition and rehabilitation. The Konkan forced the need for acquisition and implementation of path-breaking and innovative technologies that the country had not been exposed to until then. The build, operate and transfer (BOT) scheme pursued by the government continually ran into financial trouble. On top of everything, there was the aggressive deadline stipulated by the government. One can see why the Konkan project was easily the most daunting mission undertaken by the Indian Railways. From the time the mission started, and until the first whistle signalling the first train to start its journey on the line, the project had been constantly assailed by problems.

Union Minister for Railways George Fernandes discussed the revival of plans for the Konkan line with Sreedharan for the first time on 7 January 1990. There had been many serious parleys during the British Raj and later, by the numerous governments headed by the Congress party. The goal was to connect the industrial cities of southern coastal India with Bombay, the financial hub of the country, in the hope of achieving rapid acceleration of economic progress in those cities. Although the Bombay–Thane line was built in 1853 as part of the first railway project in the country, until the last decade of the twentieth century, the southern regions of Maharashtra had no rail connectivity. Plans were made in 1894, and again in 1896, to connect the region of Konkan with Mumbai, but they never materialized. During that time, Tata Sons had recommended a railway project to connect Chiplun and Bombay Port to facilitate an electrical power project utilizing the water resources of the Koyna River in the Konkan. That was rejected too, for the same reasons of project size, financial costs, etc.

When Madhu Dandavate became the minister for railways in 1977, there was a mature plan to construct a railway line down the Konkan region. But the first time plans graduated from the paper front to action was in 1989, when the Railway Budget for the year allocated Rs 62 crore to build tracks between Mangalore and Udupi. This was largely due to Railways Minister George Fernandes's desire to fulfil the dream of a Konkan railway line, following in the path of his predecessor Madhu Dandavate. Both of them were natives of the Konkan. George Fernandes was anointed with the ministership on 5 December 1989. Sreedharan was the Railway Board member engineering and ex officio secretary. Within weeks of taking charge as railways minister, George Fernandes met with the Railway Board members. He enthusiastically spoke about the two big-ticket projects he had in mind during that meeting. He said he had been mulling over them for a long time now, and that in his capacity as the minister in charge of the undertaking, he would give them top priority. He then revealed what they were. The first one was a railway bridge linking Chithoni and Boga across the Gandak River in Bihar. The second was a track along the western shoreline connecting Mangalore and Bombay. The name Konkan was not in vogue at the time. Fernandes referred to it as the West-Coast Rail line in that meeting. Having spelt his plans out, he turned towards Sreedharan and said, 'As board member, it is your duty to see to the completion of both projects. Do whatever you need to do right away.' He was publicly declaring his confidence in Sreedharan.

Two days after that conference, Sreedharan met the railways minister again. The Chithoni rail-link plan was already commissioned, the only impediment being non-allocation of the money required to begin the work. The finances had to come from four different sources—the railways, the central ministry for water resources, and the states of Bihar and Uttar Pradesh. No one was refusing funds, but they were still delaying the project. The railways was not exactly a motivated partner in this project. Their view was that it would not be worth the effort. 'To complete the project, we needed total cooperation from the two states,' Sreedharan recalled. 'The minister would have had to throw his weight around in order to rope them in.' In Sreedharan's presence, Fernandes telephoned Lalu Prasad Yadav in Bihar and Mulayam Singh Yadav in Uttar Pradesh. He explained in precise words the need to implement the project, requesting their cooperation. With that single call he had confirmed their cooperation and financial pledges. He told Sreedharan, 'There is no time to waste. On 7 January, we will inaugurate the kick-off for the project. I can do the ceremonial foundation.'

On 6 January, Sreedharan found himself with Fernandes on an official plane headed to the location of project, where the foundation ceremony was scheduled for the next day. The minister stayed at the Lucknow Raj Bhavan, while Sreedharan lodged at the railways' rest house. Next morning, Sreedharan called up the minister saying he had something important to discuss before they met at the programme location. The minister called him over to Raj Bhavan right away. When Sreedharan arrived, the minister was having breakfast. Sreedharan said, 'Today, one of your dream projects is becoming a reality. The rail bridge planned across the Gandak River has been allotted a spot that is 8 kilometres wide. This is a river that wreaks havoc every monsoon. To build the bridge, the river would have to be narrowed to only 800 metres in width. Even if we put in the greatest effort to accomplish that, the poor

Sreedharan's father, Keezhoottil Neelakantan Moosathu (left),
and mother, Elattu Valappil Kartyayini

Sreedharan in his younger days

With Radha on their wedding day

With Radha and their children

The primary school in Karukaputhur where Sreedharan studied

The Basel Evangelical Mission High School
where Sreedharan finished schooling

The wrecked Pampan Bridge after the cyclone in 1964

The rebuilding of Pampan Bridge

Radha launching *Rani Padmini*

Sreedharan at the Konkan Railway construction site

With directors during an inspection at the Konkan Railway site

At the Delhi Metro construction site

In the metro tunnel

In the driver's cabin

Receiving the Padma Vibhushan from President Pratibha Patil, 2008

Receiving a certificate of appreciation from Arai Irumi,
vice president, JICA, at the Metro Bhavan, 21 April 2010

Posing with a metro train model

With his spiritual guru, Swami Bhoomananda Tirtha

Addressing the media after the Kochi Metro announcement

Photo courtesy P.V. Sujith, *Deshabhimani*

Sreedharan at home

villagers would derive almost no benefit out of it. The poor region will not be able to take advantage of this rail line for their development needs. My opinion is that the rail bridge should be followed by another bridge for road transport.' Sreedharan appeared to have convinced the minister, who promptly called up the chief ministers of Bihar and UP again, expanding at length on the need for an additional road bridge, the budget it would require, and the respective states' roles in the projects. From what he could gather from Fernandes' conversation, Sreedharan learned that the bridge for road too would be included in the plan.

The minister arrived at the inauguration venue to lay the foundation. In the middle of his address to the dignitaries and the gathered residents of the area, he announced that the project would additionally include a bridge for road transport. This brought a burst of cheers from the local people, who were beside themselves with excitement. One of the remotest regions in the country, which did not even have basic infrastructure, was now going to be connected to the world outside. The rail bridge was completed in the year 2000, while the bridge for the road link took a little longer.

Besides making his point on the Chithoni–Boga road bridge that day, Sreedharan brought up something else too. As soon as Fernandes was finished with his phone conversation with the chief ministers, Sreedharan broached the subject of the West-Coast Rail line. He reeled out numbers and facts to the minister, telling him the project was the pragmatic need of the hour. Then he described a few aspects of the project, which needed the minister's immediate attention, in great detail. Sreedharan contended that a project of the scale of the Konkan could never be accomplished using the conventional mode of funding followed in the country. The typical funding practice was to utilize the central government's annual Railway Budget allocation to construct railway lines. It would not work in this case. Every year, the budget for all railway projects in the country stood between Rs 250 crore and Rs 300 crore annually. There were twenty to twenty-five projects underway then. When funds were allocated, each project would get hardly Rs 4–5 crore. At that rate, even immediate start of construction of the Konkan line would mean another twenty to thirty years for its completion.

That there would be unprecedented benefits for the country were this project to be completed speedily was not in question at all. Two very important steps needed to be taken—one, a new way to acquire funds for the project, and the second, creation of a special purpose vehicle (SPV) or an independent corporation to administer the construction works. Since the project would be a guaranteed financial success, there would not be much trouble finding funds from the market for it. It would be prudent for the institution overseeing the project to allow financial participation by the four states that would be the principal beneficiaries of the project. The railways could take on the principal role. Sreedharan elaborated on how every hurdle the project could possibly face could be overcome.

Having heard Sreedharan out, Fernandes readily agreed to bring the plan to the immediate attention of the prime minister, the Planning Commission and the ministry of finance for their consent. He promised action within forty-eight hours. Sreedharan wondered if this was not empty talk, but he was to be pleasantly surprised—contrary to his expectations, Fernandes had really meant what he said; he moved with great alacrity.

In exactly two days, Sreedharan got a call from Delhi. Fernandes, who had already returned to the capital from Lucknow, asked Sreedharan to meet him immediately. Fernandes seemed excited when they met. He said everything was to move exactly as outlined by Sreedharan. He had already met the Planning Board Vice Chairman Ramakrishna Hegde and Finance Minister Madhu Dandavate. All three had then jointly met Prime Minister V.P. Singh, who gave them the go-ahead. His assent was to be considered as the government's in-principle approval. And, it was time to start working on the project as the wait was over, Fernandes told Sreedharan.

Fernandes gave Sreedharan a rundown of the hectic confabulations he had had on the project over the past two days. Hegde too was from the Konkan region, and his and Fernandes's own interests in making the project happen made the railway minister's job easy. The next step was to obtain approvals from bodies like the Planning Commission. There was another hurdle—and the most important one—to cross before that, though. Cooperation from the four states still remained to be sought. Both

Fernandes and Sreedharan knew that was going to be difficult. However, they remained optimistic. Thus it was that the meeting that took place on 7 January 1990 between Sreedharan and Fernandes became a milestone in the history of the most adventurous and magnificent infrastructure mission India had ever seen.

Maharashtra, through which the major portion of the railway line would run, had Sharad Pawar as its chief minister. He was a frontline leader of the Congress party at the time. He opposed the ruling Janata Party at the centre. His cooperation could not be taken for granted. But Pawar's political differences with the centre did not turn out to be an impediment at all in this case. Sreedharan was with Fernandes when the minister telephoned Pawar. Without much ado, Pawar pledged his cooperation right away. The next call was made to Goa's chief minister, Barbosa. He too readily agreed to the plan. Kerala and Karnataka remained. Kerala had a CPI (M) government, and Karnataka was ruled by a Congress government. Fernandes had apprehensions about their assent to the project. At this point, Sreedharan asked him to leave that responsibility to him. 'It would be hard to get them to join the project because of their political allegiance. Instead, let me make some moves at the officers' level,' Sreedharan told Fernandes. The minister agreed, giving him encouragement.

Sreedharan went straight to Bangalore. He met with the Chief Secretary of the state, as well as its Secretary for Transportation. He explained to the high-ranking officers the Konkan project plan and the benefits it would bring to the state. They were instantly interested, and took him to meet Chief Minister Virendra Patil. Having heard his top officers talk excitedly about the mission, he too became enthusiastic about it. In a one-on-one meeting with Sreedharan, the chief minister promised his wholehearted cooperation to the project. Sreedharan's last destination was Trivandrum. Here too, he met the Chief Secretary and the Secretary for Transportation. The chief minister was E.K. Nayanar. Sreedharan did not have to try too hard to convince him and the two secretaries. Though Kerala was going to be a beneficiary of the project, there was not going to be an inch of the Konkan line in the state. But since it stood to get the most out of the railway line, it ought to chip in and play its part. That was the central government's view. At first glance, there seemed to be plenty of reasons for the state government to stay out of the project. But the Leftist government's approach to the Konkan was one of great approval; and, in fact, Kerala was the first official signatory to the project among the states. The way Nayanar himself pitched the benefits of the project to his state, and the swift actions that he followed it up with, filled Sreedharan with great respect for him.

Armed with the promise of support from all four states, Sreedharan made his moves very fast. He convened a meeting of the four states Chief Secretaries in Mumbai. The goal was to eliminate the rest of the obstacles in the project's way. In the meeting, they drew up the outline for the contract that the railways and the states would enter into. Sreedharan recalls the invaluable contribution of D.M. Sukthankar, Chief Secretary of Maharashtra, in drawing up the contracts. His leadership in the matter helped nip the concerns of the states; he found ways out of many a stalemate to bring about an amicable consensus.

In just about twelve days after the 7 January meeting when Sreedharan spoke to the minister, the relevant contracts had been drawn up for a large-scale, multistate project. On 19 January, the contract was signed at Karnataka Bhavan in Delhi, with the chief ministers of all the four states, their Chief Secretaries and the Railway Board members, not to mention Fernandes, in attendance. That was the first time it struck everyone that the mission was a real possibility. In the meantime, the Planning Commission too had signed its approval for the project.

That was also the year of retirement for Sreedharan, his scheduled date of retirement being 30 June. Fernandes expressed his wish to see Sreedharan take over the project, all the way to its completion. As far as Sreedharan was concerned, the Konkan project would be both a great challenge and a unique opportunity. He was well aware of the colossal responsibility that it meant too. Sreedharan was used to the well-oiled functioning of the railways, its efficiency and its strength. He had received unparalleled freedom and support from his highly skilled colleagues there. The Konkan Railway would be a far cry from it. He could see that. He would have more power for sure, as well as freedom of choice. But he would struggle for both funds and manpower. Getting well-qualified workers into the team from outside was no mean task. At the same time, there would be the unhappy prospect of objections from various quarters, and political and bureaucratic pressures along the way. Any failure would rest squarely on him. There would be no room to shift the blame. The buck would well and truly stop at his doorstep. He would have to have an answer to every question asked of him. Sreedharan thought long and hard about the good and bad aspects of the new job. In the end, he told George Fernandes he had decided to take it up, subject to one condition: the minister would have to guarantee that there would not be any external intervention or influence during the mission's planning or delivery. The mission must be completely empowered, politically and administratively. If these conditions were acceptable, then he would be more than happy to head the mission, Sreedharan told the minister. Fernandes did not need to think twice. He trusted Sreedharan. Handing over the reins to him could not be a foolhardy decision, as the mission would then have every chance of success. Fernandes told Sreedharan he would have every freedom he asked for, provided he was going to start work on the project right away.

Across Treacherous Terrains

The pristine shoreline of the Konkan, its deep forests, rugged mountains and treacherous swamps . . . all posed the greatest challenge to the physical laying of tracks. It was a brave bunch of youth riding on Bajaj's Kawasaki bikes—dream vehicles for the youngsters of the nineties—that played a significant part in the laying of the Konkan line, tracing out paths for alignment of rails for the biggest infrastructure project of the last century in India.

As soon as Sreedharan was appointed as CMD of Konkan Railway Corporation, the decision to conduct a new survey of the terrain was taken. It was not as easy as it appeared to be. In fact, the task was downright dangerous. Many places along the route had no connectivity at all. No vehicle could get anywhere. Into this situation rode the Kawasaki bikers. Around 400 youth, fresh out of engineering colleges, took up the challenge with the support of Kawasaki. Where regular vehicles could not reach, the Kawasakis would venture, hauling levelling instruments and other equipment across rugged and remote locations.

These Kawasakis were specially made to negotiate rough terrain. Fuel for the bikes, and an allowance of Rs 100 a day kept this young battalion going. The 'bikees', as they were called, completed the task much earlier than anticipated.

Konkan Railway Corporation Ltd (KRCL) was registered on 19 July 1990. Before Sreedharan's retirement, the Public Enterprises Selection Board (PESB) had designated him to the leadership of the Konkan Railway. The minister for railways announced his appointment, which had the consent of the central ministers. Sreedharan took charge on 30 July. The first thing he did was to prepare a new report immediately, although another report from Southern Railway had been submitted earlier. The alignment based on Southern Railway's survey had many shortcomings. It had listed many densely populated locations which could have been avoided. It also had numerous technical flaws. The ministry for railways had ordered an engineering survey for rail transportation down the southern coast in 1984. In 1985, the survey, covering 325 kilometres between Mangalore and Madgaon was completed, the success of which became an inspiration to the surveyors to extend it to cover the rest of the Konkan coast. In the end, the report was submitted to the ministry. Pointing to the limitations of the survey, Sreedharan began a new survey. Ever since talks of reviving plans for the Konkan Railway route had begun to brew, there were several studies and surveys done at various stages. The earliest study for the line between Bombay and Goa was done sometime in the seventies. In 1971–72, Southern

Railway had done studies for a line between Mangalore
and Bombay. A detailed survey was done in 1975–77 for
the line between Dasgaon and Ratnagiri. The railways'
survey in 1984–85 was based on all the surveys and studies
that had been conducted earlier.

Upon Sreedharan's instructions, KRCL conducted two
surveys, one along the shore and another along the inland
area. Based on that, technical modifications were made
to the plan in order that the lines could join the existing
rail lines at both terminals. Thus, the shortcomings of the
earlier surveys were rectified, and a new plan acceptable
to a wider population was delivered. The region through
which the line would run stretched from south to north,
with the Western Ghats to the east and the Arabian Sea
to the west. It was vastly diverse. The countless rivers
originating from the ghats and flowing eastwards, the
riverbanks, the swamps and the forests made Konkan an
inaccessible fortress. The steep mountain ranges of the
ghats and the dense jungles were difficult to access. It was
only after many valiant efforts that the prospect of laying
rail lines across them was deemed possible.

The new alignment went through the districts of
Raigad, Ratnagiri and Sindhudurg in Maharashtra, the
South and West districts of Goa, and the Uttara and
Dakshina Kannada districts of Karnataka. The track that
began from Roha in Maharashtra, passed 70 kilometres to
cross Panvel and passed five towns including Madgaon-
Vir of Raigad district, to enter the coastal towns of Alibag
and Murud of Ratnagiri district. The Raigad Fort, which

had belonged to Chhatrapati Shivaji, a Maratha warrior of the seventeenth century, stood within shouting distance from the future rail line. The stretch of 210 kilometres in Ratnagiri was the most difficult, and took a lot out of everyone at KRCL. The many rivers, rivulets, rapids, mountain ranges, forests, and the peculiar soil posed all kinds of challenges. The major towns here were Chiplun, Khed and Sangameshwar. Sindhudurg district had the towns of Kankavali, Kudal and Sawantwadi. Goa, whose major source of income was tourism, threw the project off its path many times. The Uttara and Dakshina Kannada districts of Karnataka ran right along the coast, the latter being very thickly populated. The rivers from the Western Ghats and the mountains from which they flowed were intimidating in equal measure. The ghats rose 600–1800 metres above sea level and appeared to be insurmountable. Geographically, it probably presented the most forbidding picture anywhere in the country for a railway line, clearly the reason why one had not been laid all these decades. The new survey and alignment actually cut the distance between Roha and Mangalore by 77 kilometres, and provided for more tunnels and bridges to fill the gaps. The original distance by rail from Mangalore to Bombay had been 2041 kilometres; Konkan pulled it back to 914 kilometres, saving 1127 kilometres of journey. The Mangalore–Ahmedabad route would be only 1295 kilometres now, and the Mangalore–Delhi rail journey would be 764 kilometres shorter. Cochin would get closer to Bombay by 514 kilometres. The Bombay–Mangalore journey would take twenty-six hours instead of forty-one. Kochi–Bombay passengers were set to save twelve hours, and Goa-bound travellers from Bombay, ten hours.

Sreedharan began to scout for personnel to build his team for the project. KRCL was headquartered in Navi Mumbai. Sreedharan especially took time to gather technologists from centres of technology such as the Indian Railways, National Hydroelectric Power Corporation, etc. KRCL's recruitment advertisements inviting technical candidates for a career with them brought unexpected response. Even though the project had sweat and blood written all over it, Sreedharan's presence at the helm had its charm for the applicants. V. Anand, an engineer who joined the Konkan Railway, recalled how he was discouraged by his supervisor at his earlier job, who advised him not to join a project that could potentially be a disaster. Disregarding conventional wisdom, Anand decided to join what he saw as an adventure. Sreedharan hired him as a mechanical engineer, and later as vigilance officer. Sreedharan personally vetted the applications in the selection process. The only criteria considered were suitable qualifications, skills and previous job experience.

Below the CMD in the organization were the Chief Secretaries of the four states, the directors for finance, projects and technology, the Railway Board's representatives, and additional members to take care of works, budget, traffic and planning. The total cost of the project was estimated at Rs 3375 crore, out of which the railways would pay Rs 408 crore. The state of Maharashtra would bring in Rs 176 crore, Goa and Kerala Rs 48 crore each, and Karnataka Rs 120 crore. The rest of the funds had to come in the form of taxable and non-taxable bonds from the domestic financial market.

Sreedharan and his team had determined to pace the project at the fastest they could by employing the best technology available in the world. This was perhaps the first decision taken about choice of technology. The target was to build tracks to allow train speeds of 160 kilometres per hour. But tracks alone could not ensure that; the quality of trains had to match. In fact, there was no train in the country operating at that speed during the time of the Konkan project. The decision to build faster tracks had considered the possibility of faster trains in the future. Currently, the average speed of trains on the Konkan line is 105 kilometres per hour.

In the meantime, preparatory works for the projects were being done without a pause. Everything was moving fast. Sreedharan met with a few contractors who had been working with the railways in Mangalore. He let them know that the paperwork would take a couple of months more to finish at the office of KRCL, but they had to get to work right away. Now, this was not a practice the railways was known for. Quite possibly, this would invite audit objections. Knowing Sreedharan's methods and style of functioning, however, the contractors, on their part, trusted him completely. They began the work earnestly without even a shred of paper to show for confirmation of their contracts. If, so far, they had been doing business ranging in lakhs of rupees, this time they were undertaking projects of the order of crores of rupees, staking everything they had, solely based on their trust in Sreedharan.

The chief minister of Maharashtra, Sharad Pawar, laid the foundation for the construction works on 15 September 1990. Admittedly, the Konkan project was by far the most difficult railway project in India. The closest comparison could be the Assam Rail Link, which was constructed on a war footing, the focus being the speed with which it was required to be delivered. The Assam Rail Link project was to connect the state of Assam, after the partition of the country, to the mainland, which was only possible with the help of a rail link. The losses to the Indian Railways resulting from the Partition was colossal. North Eastern Railway's Bengal–Assam line went to Pakistan. Two very important workshops were lost as well. The major hub of rail transportation in north India happened to be in Karachi. To partly compensate for these losses, the plan was to build the strategically vital Assam Rail Link on a war footing. The army's technical skills were used to the fullest to achieve this goal. Within two years, 228 kilometres of track were laid. The all-important project was done under the leadership of Karnail Singh, who later became a Railway Board member. The Konkan did not present the urgency or the historical context of the Assam Rail Link project. That it was finished on schedule—and in keeping with quality parameters—with no external motivation at all was highly appreciated by a grateful nation.

While the ground works for the Konkan project got kicking on higher gears, there was trouble brewing on the political front that could potentially derail the project itself. The tests visited upon the project from its start to finish would have deterred lesser people. The Janata Dal government at the centre fell in October 1990, raising the spectre of an imminent demise for the project. It had happened as a matter of course, there being a lead up to it that played out over a week's time. George Fernandes, who had been nurturing the Konkan project like his baby, was not the minister for railways any more. There was disquiet and apprehension as to what direction the project would take. As for Sreedharan, his heart and soul were in the Konkan mission. He saw it as an opportunity to offer everything he had assimilated and learned over his decades with the railways for the benefit of the country. The political storm at the Centre had everyone on edge about the future of the project. Sreedharan did not lose hope. In the end, none of the fears about the project came true. The new government that took over simply pledged its support to the project.

Curiously, the new minister for railways, Jaffer Sharief, announced in Parliament that the Konkan project would be completed in five years when, at that point, only preliminary surveys had been done. Approximately 43,000 families had been estimated to be relocated on account of land acquisitions for the project. Only after that could Sreedharan's team start marking the lands for construction work to begin. All the bridges and tunnels across the

treacherous terrain still remained to be built. That too
in just five years now! The unilateral announcement in
Parliament put the Konkan team in a real bind.

The alignment had been finally drawn up with the
help of satellites. The next huge challenge was to move
residents out of the project areas and acquire the required
lands from the owners. The team members approached
the 43,000 families whose lands had to be acquired,
with a positive pitch on the benefits of the project. Then
they inquired about the specific issues related to each
individual that would hold them back from parting
with their land. No stone was left unturned to provide
them credible promise that each of their issues would be
addressed swiftly. Working among the inhabitants of the
region helped the team gain confidence. 'Give us your
land and relocate to a place you'd like to move to. Build
another house and live in a rented home until it's done.
Whatever might be the expense, the Konkan team would
recompense you within a year and a half,' people were told.
The home owners could even dismantle their own houses,
and pick up anything they wanted to take along from
there. The rehabilitation policy appeared very generous
even at a casual glance. Each of these measures blunted
the typical negativity that pervades among any population
facing unexpected displacement for development projects
of this scale. When the resistance in Goa brewed to a boil,
youngsters who were sent on motorcycles to spread positive
tidings about the new railway line found goodwill among
even the detractors. In about nine to eight months, all the

hard work the team had put in began to bear incredible results. KRCL had acquired all the lands it needed for the project, though there was now a deluge of court cases to deal with. Yet, overcoming the first hurdle of finding land for the length of track to be laid out was in itself a stellar achievement.

Under normal circumstances, land acquisition, especially for basic infrastructure development projects, would should mean a long-drawn process that consumes a lot of precious time. The state governments would take their time acquiring the lands, following their laborious legal framework every step of the way. The reason why land acquisition was speedily accomplished on the Konkan and Delhi Metro projects was not because the state governments pushed harder, but because of Sreedharan's policy of transparent and direct contact which yielded the desired results. While the governments had lumbered along, brandishing land acquisition laws in 1984, Sreedharan and his colleagues laid out a plan to overcome the complex maze of the law. Critics could say that his plans were not prudent or that some of his actions were downright illegal. Inviting tenders for construction on a property which had not been released from due process technically made for operating outside of the law. Those who had learnt to prize the value of time would agree that waiting forever, on the other hand, could be no less foolhardy. However, groups with special interests could very well criticize Sreedharan's approach to legal technicalities and block his mission, which we have seen as recently as with the Kochi project, where the devious collusion of such forces got them tactical victories.

The Leftist government in Kerala, which was in power until 2011, had wanted DMRC, led by Sreedharan, to build the metro for Kochi. When the Congress returned to power, change in the political balance and interests was a given, and Sreedharan did not pay attention to it as he went ahead with the tender invitation process to build a rail yard in Aluva before the Kochi Metro Rail Limited (KMRL) had formally signed the contracts. The land had not been acquired from the owners yet. KMRL Managing Director Tom Jose shot off a letter questioning the action, and demanded that all activities be stopped immediately, bringing the entire machinery to a grinding halt. The special interest group's tactic set off a chain of unexpected events, starting with local resistance to land acquisitions, which had never happened until then. This development had the effect of an emergency brake applied on the project, which had been poised to gain momentum. It took another ten months before DMRC could even resume work on the same tender. Throwing rule books at honest and efficient workers gained nothing more than a gross loss of ten months!

Sreedharan took a humanistic approach to the land acquisition process. He knew confrontations and legal battles could only mean loss of precious time. He had no doubt that those who let go of their home and lands must get the justice and empathy they deserved. But, under normal circumstances, acquisition of lands would take a long time to complete. That could not be allowed to dictate the course of the project either. The Konkan team's solution was to get signed documents from the land owners pledging the transfer of their assets in the presence of revenue authorities. As soon as this document was done, work could begin. The legal process could take its course in parallel. In this way, Sreedharan and his team could save invaluable time. Those who were displaced received compensation for their home and lands based on existing market rates. Additionally, they received assistance for relocation, the Konkan team ignoring any pressure all this may put on the project budget. Trees lost were paid for too, mango and jackfruit trees bringing in compensation of Rs 2000 each. Items such as window frames, roof materials, etc. from the houses being torn down were allowed to be taken away for free. Places of worship were intentionally avoided in laying the alignment. People of poor means who were rehabilitated were given perks, including relocation assistance.

The people of Amaywada lost access to a public well when the Pernem tunnel was dug. The Konkan team simply dug another well for them. Yet another well was dug in Chapdi, a village near Vir. The team had gifted wells, pipes, culverts and roads to the people of Mahad. There was also an incident when an entire portion of a cemetery was lifted over to Dasgaon. The cemetery was at a place where the rivers of Kal, Savitri and Nageshwari met; it had existed for generations, and was considered a holy place where the forefathers of the natives had been laid to eternal rest. However, aligning the tracks to avoid the cemetery was impossible. Obliterating the cemetery, of course, was unthinkable. Finally, the project authorities promised the local residents they would find another location for the cemetery. Everything that remained in the cemetery would be relocated to the new one, and a new, paved road would be laid to it. As soon as the villagers had given their nod, the team went to work, moving the remains of the departed and all the memorial stones, until the last shard of cherished rock was shifted to the new cemetery. All the expenses were paid for by KRCL.

The total area of land acquired for the project was 4850 hectares. In all, 43,000 families had to be displaced. The home and land owners' compensation cost was about Rs 144 crore. Going by the history and practice of displacement and rehabilitation in India and the tardiness of its legal system, acquisition of land on this scale would have taken one hundred years. The Konkan team got more than half of the land it needed, well within the first year of KRCL's inception.

Ten Commandments

Sreedharan's much-acclaimed practice of working to 'reverse clocks' during the time of the Delhi Metro's construction was originally introduced in the Konkan project. The clocks that ran backwards were brought in as part of a conscious decision to get the construction works done according to a predetermined schedule. These clocks, which were present at every office space and project site, watched over and reminded everyone of the value of each passing minute. Sreedharan took the clocks with him to Kochi too for his metro mission there. It was fascinating to hear Sreedharan narrate the story of how the reverse clocks ended up with him. He was once asked a question on his project management techniques that reaped such wonderful rewards. The question that followed was on whether he had copied from other techniques employed on big-ticket projects elsewhere. Sreedharan replied that the only technique he had ever copied was the idea of reverse clocks, and went on to talk about the origin of this habit. In the beginning of the 1980s, a huge iron mine operating in the region of Kudremukh was being worked on to meet an unprecedented growth in exports of iron ore. Excavation was being done at an accelerated pace at Prime Minister Indira Gandhi's behest. Having been given specific targets, Mukul Chand Khanna, a reputed engineer, decided to install reverse clocks at the site. This had come to Sreedharan's notice during his time at the railways. When he accepted the Konkan mandate, he decided to adopt the idea for his project. In fact, he went to Delhi to meet Khanna at his residence, to discuss the practice and its benefits. Khanna vouched for the effectiveness of the gadget with glowing testimonials. That was how hundreds of reverse clocks found their way to the offices and work sites of the Konkan Railway.

If we analyse the overall execution of the Konkan project, the greatest feat of all was the fast delivery of a world-class piece of railway infrastructure. The reason earlier attempts at the project had hit a wall at the planning stage itself was its apparent impracticality. The many surveys that followed, one after another, estimated the project would take long and painful years to accomplish. Southern Railway's report had suggested at least ten years. The story of each of the larger projects in the country did not suggest otherwise either. If we exclude projects that were done under special circumstances such as the Assam Rail Link, it was discernibly clear that the success of the Konkan mission could be attributed to the core principles of project management followed by Sreedharan and his team. Before we get into the details of the adventure-filled construction of the Konkan Railway, we need to delve a little deeper into the design, features and strategy of the delivery systems adopted for the project.

The only way to complete the project within the allocated time was to do the hard work harder. Sreedharan knew the need of the hour was agile and transparent project management. He put in thoughtful efforts to overcome the difficulties and shortcomings he had faced at various junctures during his time at the railways. Everyone in the team had to know what their specific role was and how much time was left to fulfil what was expected of them. Each member must possess the dedication needed to strive towards the goal. With this in mind, he formulated a set of corporate directions focused on ten major points. The first was installation of the reverse clocks. In reality, the reverse clocks displayed shorter schedules than the actual allotted time on the books. The presence of reverse clocks gave team members a sense of time ticking away, motivating them to head for their goals without delay.

Sreedharan created a small but highly functional team of top management. The KRCL board vested the highest authority in the hands of its managing director. Legal procedures to select officers and technical employees were followed rigorously under Sreedharan's supervision. Significantly, the most important qualities required in a member of his team for the Konkan project were strength of character and honesty. Beyond educational qualifications and experience on the job, each candidate's conduct in his or her official capacity was reviewed threadbare. Regardless of the scale of talent and other qualifications, should there be any doubt about a candidate's integrity in his past, he would be overlooked for the position right away. As a result of this, the Konkan project acquired a lean and agile team in its leadership. The team had decided they would not micromanage daily activities at the lower levels. Making those who had been delegated the responsibility accountable would suffice. The top management confined their focus to security, design, management, contract payments and advice on strategically significant decisions. In the same way that chief engineers of each zone were given powers, employees under them too had been given powers relevant to their roles. The intent was to empower employees to take decisions and avoid the culture of dependency on superiors in trivial matters. Not having to rely on the corporate office for their daily activities helped employees down the line move the project much faster.

The Konkan Railway had to pass through seven revenue districts spread across three states. Sreedharan's next step was to assign the seven districts to seven zones. They were Mahad, Ratnagiri North, Ratnagiri South, Kudal, Panaji, Karwar and Udupi. Each zone would have a chief engineer to oversee the project's progress in the zone's domain. Sreedharan handed over powers to them after dividing up the 760-kilometre line into zones covering 100–120 kilometres each. His logic for this was simple. Each district had a revenue officer in the designation of district collector, and a police superintendent for law enforcement. All issues could be resolved locally by the person to whom the zone was allotted. Another reason was that completing several 100–120 kilometre stretches in parallel in five years' time appeared a much more achievable target to the mind than a 760-kilometre stretch in the same period. Barring unforeseen issues, the project would be on course to make it to the finish line in five years.

Another major strategy was to connect all seven zones to an effective communication grid. In those times, communication infrastructure was not very well developed. Even the major cities did not have moderately reliable—let alone the best of class—communication systems yet. Effective communications being a non-negotiable requirement for the project, KRCL rented out a line from the department of telecommunications (DoT) for themselves. Phone and fax lines were installed, linking all seven chief engineers' offices. A network of computer systems was set up. The chief engineers could now get all the relevant information they wanted, and send and receive messages promptly and effectively.

Yet another step Sreedharan took was to restructure financial transactions for the project. As far as the Indian Railways was concerned, this was the most important process of all. All activities in the railways depended on the department of finance, rendering the section a bottleneck and the reason for routine delay of many of the railways' enterprises. Although the railways were justifiably capable of decisive schedules, the criticism that their finance department had not been as keen to see their projects accomplished as it was to wield the purse strings, was an established fact. In the light of his own decades of experience at the railways, Sreedharan promised himself that such a tradition would not take root in the new enterprise under his watch. He prepared himself for a major overhaul, akin to a revolution in conventional financial practice. He had not given special powers to the finance officers at KRCL, as they had been in the railways. On the other hand, those who had real powers were the officers in other departments. They would take the decisions. The finance department could advise them on financial matters only if it was necessary. There was no room for unsolicited intervention or obstructive arguments on their part. He brought the best finance officers from the railways into his project. Soon, the structural reforms proved to be most practical, and bore considerably beneficial results. It was also noted that there was no friction between the finance officers and others over the course of the project.

The emphasis in the Konkan team was on collective action based on mutual trust. To facilitate such a culture, papers and files were avoided in everyday activities wherever possible. Every Monday, in Sreedharan's presence, the project's progress would be reviewed. The head of every department would attend the meeting. The first meeting of every month would include all the engineers too. All aspects related to project delivery were discussed at that meeting. The heads of each department would go over the previous week's plan to review progress and shortfalls. The final item on the agenda would be planning for the upcoming week. The interesting fact about these meetings was that their minutes or the decisions taken were never recorded. Sreedharan deliberately chose not to do that, as part of his reforms. He considered such practices as nothing more than a waste of time. Everyone involved in the project knew precisely what was going on at the workplace on a daily basis. They need not be told what they were supposed to be doing in the first place. What benefit would it bring to the table when you spend time and resource documenting the activities that are already being done anyway? Sreedharan's rationale for the policies and practices he lay down won him his colleagues' trust, encouraged voluntary accountability, filled them with enthusiasm for work, and brought them a quiet confidence. Above all, there was great team spirit all around.

The next item in focus related to the contractors, who were responsible for the formidable construction works for the Konkan. Sreedharan and his colleagues knew that a project of this nature depended heavily on the contractors' performance. The Konkan was a railway project, and it went without saying that civil construction works would always be fraught with danger. The contractors' role in facing up to the dangers and overcoming difficulties would be paramount. The selection of candidates for contract jobs was therefore done with utmost care.

Not all contractors were invited to tender for the jobs. At the same time, Sreedharan made sure those who had proven their skills and efficiency would be with the project. Contractors such as Vellappally Constructions, Cherian Varkey, etc. were some of them. Vellappally had been personally asked to cooperate on this project. A shortlist of potential contractors was drawn up before the invite was even sent to them. The contractors' work history, style of functioning and capabilities were researched for the shortlist. The final recipients of the contracts were chosen from among the list. The contracts contained generous conditions, and a system of advance payment, which was instantly acceptable to the contracting companies. Construction jobs were given to contractors who had stellar records in the country, such as Afcons, L&T, Gammon India, etc.

If contractors could not be paid in time, progress of the construction works would be blocked. Then there was the importance of giving them timely and proper instructions, without which the best of them would fail to deliver. These were the lessons Sreedharan had learnt from his three-decade term at the railways. He made sure timely decisions were made to help the contractors perform their work without a hitch, no matter how complex the issue, and even if it required the CMD himself to weigh in. His colleagues and contractors could recall several occasions when Sreedharan himself travelled miles to facilitate the decision-making process. So many tunnels and bridges were being built at the same time, and many verdicts and opinions were being tossed about for consideration all the time. To push the jobs on all fronts needed effort on a very great scale. The promise to contractors that no decision would take more than forty-eight hours ever was one that was set in stone.

Decisions were taken on the spot when it was so required. The fast and unambiguous directions that came as a result of the process Sreedharan had set in helped accelerate the project's progress. P. Sreeram, who had been with Sreedharan since 1970, recalled an incident during his time at Konkan. Construction of a major tunnel was on, and as the work progressed, the machine got stuck in a huge rock. Sreeram explained the situation to the CMD, who happened to be at the site. There was no option but to stop the day's work, except if another tunnel was bored to remove the rock, Sreeram suggested. 'Then we are doing it,' Sreedharan said. Sreeram was not sure when he could start working on the second tunnel. 'Right now!' Sreedharan responded as though this question should never have been raised. Sreeram's apprehensions were about the approval and budget needed for the additional work. He told Sreedharan so. 'That should never be an issue. Let me worry about it. What's worse would be halting the work. Time is precious. Do not delay. Let's begin.' As soon as Sreedharan finished his sentence, the machinery began to hum and charge to work. That was Sreedharan's style of functioning.

Sreedharan was particular about paying the contractors on time. A new deal was introduced in the billing process, one distinctly different from the procedures followed in the railways. His reform was to let the contractors measure their own work and prepare their bills. The bills thus prepared by the contractors would get them at least 75 per cent of the amount within forty-eight hours. The rest of the bill would be paid in about a week's time, after the inspections. Typically, industrial practice was for contractors to be paid 10–15 per cent as advance. Because of this, the contractors not only never had to worry about not getting paid, they also cherished the fact that they were being valued and trusted for the role they played in the historic mission.

Once every month, the contractors would be invited to a meeting. Sreedharan would be present at these meetings. When large tunnels had to be excavated or the latest technology employed for a construction job, these meetings were especially useful, as the issues and concerns of the contractors would be heard out and resolutions worked upon, improving the contractors' overall efficiency. In the initial phases, there was massive consumption of cement, iron rods and explosives. Getting these materials on time would often mean a legally knotty affair. Items such as explosives were bought directly by the corporation. Sreedharan and his team did not adopt a policy of strict adherence to the book. Their goal was to finish the mission by the deadline. For that reason, the contractors never had to confront the problems they did on typical government projects. The team listened carefully to their issues, and as soon as they were convinced of their substance, undoing the knots for them would be the priority. For instance, when inflation was skyrocketing, the amount paid became insufficient for the contractors who were working on a few of the tunnels. Having been convinced of their arguments' validity, Sreedharan agreed to review their rates. In the larger interest of the corporation, though, he negotiated

with them. On certain occasions, he had to go beyond
the agreements in the original contracts. However, none
of those actions raised a single doubter's brow. What
was more important was that these actions, considering
the circumstances which called for them, were beyond
reproach.

It has been mentioned earlier that the major portion of
the land needed to lay the tracks had been already acquired
by KRCL. Construction work too had been started on the
acquired lands. Although the activities were being done
at an accelerated pace, core rules and regulations were
always followed. However, the process was not entirely
immune to the undesirable machinations of influential
sources. Sreedharan confronted them head-on. When a
senior official attempted to intervene on behalf of certain
contractors—his eye being on a contract for one of the
major portions of the line—Sreedharan did not yield.
He followed regular process to invite tenders for the job
and awarded the contract to the company that quoted the
lowest bid. This was an act of defiance against the senior
official. What was more interesting was that the directors
of the Railway Board who represented the Indian Railways
in KRCL stood behind the official, who, sensing their
support, decided to continue with his shenanigans. His
calculation was that if he could garner support from a
majority on the KRCL board, Sreedharan's decision could
be overturned. He nominated three more members to the
board who could be expected to support him. They would
move before the board a proposal to cancel the contract

which had been awarded, and begin a new process to invite
tenders for the same job. Having seen through the sinister
plan, Sreedharan stayed away from the board meeting. As
he had foreseen, the board, in the absence of the CMD,
cancelled the awarded contract and decided to call for a
new tender.

Sreedharan did not let this pass. In company law, the
CMD had special powers to review any decision taken
by the board in his absence, and cancel it if required.
Sreedharan employed this provision. He called a meeting
and announced that the decision taken in his absence
was being annulled. He followed it up by sending a letter
to the ministry for railways, saying that if the ministry's
interest in cancelling and inviting the tender was
supremely important, it should please let the CMD and
the board know of that officially in writing. That was a
lightning bolt from him. In the Companies Act, there
was a provision for that too. The Railway Board could
indeed ask to overlook the CMD's decision and reinstate
the resolution. The CMD was obliged to submit to it.
But there was one problem. Such an instruction would
have to come straight to the board from the minister
of railways, with his signature on it—a process called
'presidential directive'. Processing of the original tender
had already been done. Cancelling that and inviting
another meant a lot of overheads in terms of money and
time. Unless it was done under exceptional cases, and
for valid reasons, there would definitely be objections
in the audit, KRCL being a public-sector organization.

Sreedharan's ace won the game for him. There was no response from the ministry to his letter.

In September 1994, Sreedharan summoned all heads of departments at KRCL to his cabin. Anand, who then headed the mechanical department, recalled Sreedharan's narration of the story of the contract and the minister's attempt to intervene, as well as his unambiguous announcement that if the situation were to deteriorate any further, he would not hesitate to resign from his position. The entire posse of heads of departments voiced their support to Sreedharan. They declared they would stand behind his decisions and declared too that if he had to go, none of them would continue on the project. Eventually, events unfolded the way Sreedharan had hoped they would. Anand believed that the political leadership could not have taken any other direction. It was not easy to boot out a proven technocrat like Sreedharan; neither was it easy to replace him. The government, having been convinced of the facts, could not have made any move that would not have been suicidal, Anand pointed out.

New Tracks, a New Line

If you ask whether the Iraq–Kuwait war in 1991 could, in any way, be associated with the Konkan mission, the answer would be yes. The war broke out when the mission was poised to progress by leaps and bounds. The country faced its worst fuel scarcity. Operations on many major projects had ceased because of the acute fuel shortage in the country on account of the war. That the Konkan project did not stop, or even slow down for that matter, was unusual, and another great example of how well the team had prepared to enter the operations phase of the historic mission. Hundreds of vehicles had to run up and down between the construction sites of the Konkan. To provide them fuel at convenient locations, fuel procurement had already been done at petrol bunks in appropriate volumes. When the whole world suffered the impact of a sudden war, which stalled many projects, work on the Konkan progressed as usual. It was not as though the Konkan team had special powers to predict the future, but it all came down to basic planning and dedicated hard work that ensured enough stocks of fuel to support the project. A simple act of farsightedness allowed the Konkan to continue work unimpeded even during the greatest fuel famine of our time.

Sreedharan and team had entered the operations phase of the project, for which they had meticulously planned and prepared. One of them has been described already. By the time the designs for the tunnels, culverts and bridges were completed, the tender schedules too were ready. The list of supplementary agencies was compiled with the guidance of Asian Development Bank and World Bank. The final decisions were made within seventy-two hours of acceptance of the tenders for construction of tunnels and bridges. Four plants were installed—in Chiplun, Kudal, Madgaon and Murudeswar—in order to haul ten-and-a-half lakh concrete sleepers to their respective sites on schedule. Provisions were made for enough stocks of steel and cement at the sites. On top of all that, to assure highest quality of delivery, an independent agency of international repute was commissioned. Systems for the medical and vigilance sections were laid down with elaborate care. As a consequence, the Konkan project was lauded at international forums for its rigorous standards of quality. In the June 1995 edition of *The Civil Engineer International*, author David Howard wrote that India as a nation had crossed a major milestone in railway infrastructure development with the Konkan, where the largest and most adventurous construction of a railway line was underway.

Sreedharan and his colleagues replicated the success of the groundbreaking reforms they had ushered in at the administrative and managerial levels, to project delivery as well. They utilized every technology and skill available in the country and abroad to achieve their goal. Every inch of the new line, from start to finish, saw challenges cropping up, in the shape of a bridge or a tunnel or a culvert. Each had been overcome by the team, with the resourceful and pragmatic use of the engineering and management tools at their disposal. The Konkan Railway's logo *had* to be a tunnel with railway tracks—a symbol of its never-say-die spirit—as tunnels were what had put the project to the sternest test. It was because of the large number of tunnels on the route that the alignment, originally estimated at 837 kilometres, could be shortened by 27 kilometres. In the final alignment, the track length under tunnels increased to 75 kilometres! Later, a few steep culverts had to be converted into tunnels, taking the final number of tunnels to 92 and their total length to 84.8 kilometres—or, roughly 11 per cent of the total length of the tracks.

Digging into the belly of towering mountains to carve tunnels into them under the ever-present danger of falling rocks and mudslides was never going to be a trivial matter. The constant threat of mishap lurked every step of the way. The technology and machinery available in the country were never going to be a match to this gargantuan task. Sreedharan and his team prepared to travel around the globe to get appropriate machinery for the mission. Under the deputy chief mechanical engineer's lead, a panel of experts visited a few countries and came up with a list of supplier companies, from which Atlas Copco from Switzerland was selected to supply the latest, specialized machinery for the tunnels. The Swiss government financed the import of the expensive machinery at zero interest rate. It took a lot of effort to even bring the equipment to the sites. Swedish experts too had arrived at the site to commission them. V. Anand, chief mechanical engineer at KRCL, recalled how a huge section of officers was sceptical, and kept away from the new technology until the contractors had put them to good use and showed them the results. As work progressed on the tunnels, providing them with lighting and ventilation was nothing short of hard toil. KRCL agreed to lend the equipment they had bought to the contractors to use for free. But there was one condition—the work had to be done on schedule. Every single day's delay past the deadline would be added to the rental bill due from the contractor. These seemingly magnanimous offers were not done at the contractors' behest. The task being uniquely challenging, Sreedharan and his team had to recommend appropriate machinery to the contractors. The heads of departments at KRCL used Sreedharan's influence and contacts in the government to avail themselves of any assistance needed from the state.

The Karbude tunnel near Ratnagiri was the longest in the network. The 6506-metre tunnel was, in fact, the longest in the subcontinent. The Natuwadi tunnel was 4389 metres long, and the Tike and Bardewadi tunnels 4077 metres and 4000 metres respectively. It was more dangerous to dig tunnels through loose dirt than through rocky hills. There was no technology or equipment designed for such terrain. The last one to be built, the Pernem tunnel in Maharashtra, was in such a precarious location bounded by a topography of quicksand, that loose soil kept falling down during the course of construction. As soon as some digging was done, loose dirt would begin to cascade down into the length of tunnel that had been dug, which would then collapse. Twenty workers lost their lives in accidents during its perilous construction. Water and mud would repeatedly cause cave-ins, blocking progress on the tunnel many times. The 1.5-kilometre stretch of tunnel, on which work started in 1992, took five years to finish. The endless tests at Pernem added five months to the overall completion of the project. The 2.5-kilometre Parchuri tunnel had a different story to tell. As the excavation happened, water would spout in as though it were blood spurting out of a deep wound. The Byndoor tunnel under the NH 17 had caused landslides, forcing traffic on the road to find alternative routes till the tunnel was completed. A dozen tunnels, including the ones at Bhatkal, Honavar, Paadi, Verna, Old Goa and Savarde, posed great dangers to the workers. Their refusal to yield to setbacks, and their constant adoption of newer technologies to overcome the setbacks, held the team in good stead through every circumstance at work.

Many bridges built for the Konkan line broke records in terms of size. The yawning valley of Ratnagiri where Alphonso mangoes grew, saw the tallest bridge in

Asia—the Panvelnadi bridge—come up. To the west of this tall scaffolding lay the 1.1-kilometre Banewadi tunnel and to its south, the 4-kilometre Tike tunnel. The length of the Ratnagiri valley was more than 500 metres and its depth ranged from 50 metres to 64 metres. The tall pillars were hardened using a technology known as 'slip form'. Although the technology was available in the country, this was the first time it was put to use. The bridge could not have been built without the efficient and accurate application of the technology. Indian consultants led the work, but under the capable supervision of a German agency. When its construction was completed, the Panvelnadi bridge, at its highest point, was only 4 metres shorter than the Qutub Minar. The bridge bagged the American Concrete Institute's Award for exceptional construction in concrete in 1995. It also received an award from the Indian Institute of Bridge Engineers.

We have discussed the Konkan tracks' capacity to support trains travelling at 160 kilometres an hour. Many modern technologies were employed to realize that goal. One of them was the 'incremental launching' technique. Konkan used the technique in the country for the first time. The novel technology was needed to install giant viaducts. It was impossible to support and bolt large viaducts on top of dizzyingly tall pillars. A new technique had to be explored to hoist the viaducts on to the pillars. The 'incremental launching' technique adopted by the Konkan engineers consisted of building whole decks and hoisting each of them sideways till they reached the other side.

Imagine hauling box girders that weighed approximately 12,500 tonnes over a great height! The first such deck to be installed was in Panvel. It was 420 metres long. Sreedharan used the technique in the Delhi Metro project too.

Another technique used was 'ballast-less track construction'. This was a technology to secure tracks without the support of frames. Sreedharan tried this for the tracks in the tunnels. When it became clear that the regular process of laying tracks would not work, Sreedharan instructed his engineers to adopt this technique. It had later become a signature innovation coming out of the Konkan experience. The attraction of this technique was that it would not later require the chore of constant maintenance. 'Turnout' in railway parlance referred to any point where a train would leave the main track and enter a loop line. The Konkan Railway's use of 'speed turnouts' proved to be a turning point in technology adoption. Trains now could pass these turnouts at speeds as high as 50 kilometres per hour. On other tracks, the maximum speed possible at turnouts was 15 kilometres per hour. Every bridge, except three spans, had tracks laid using the ballast technique. Two of these spans stood over the Zuari River in Goa and the third span was across the Mandovi River. Since vessels in the rivers had to pass under the bridges, steel girders had been installed for the tracks. Here was an innovation that bore Sreedharan's unmistakable touch. Steel girders of a triangular shape had been used in the country for the first time. The total length of the girders was 125 metres. Another first in the country was the use of Teflon bearings in steel girders that reduced friction considerably. The bearings were designed specifically for the project.

The longest of all the Konkan Bridges would be the link across the Sharavati River. Being close to the sea, the river threw extreme dangers to the team when they built the bridge over it. The 2.06-kilometre bridge had to be built on a natural swampland filled with sand and dense mud, which the team found an incredibly hard task. The 288 pillars in the river had to be on piles at depths that ranged from 15 metres to 40 metres. Each pillar rose on top of four to six piles. As was the practice, construction of the piles and the concreting were done utilizing modern technologies. Twenty girders weighing approximately 400 tonnes each were hoisted above the river with the help of a large barge and a dredger. The construction works of the Konkan carry their own histories of human adventure, but, strewn down the length of the Konkan Railway line, one can see many awe-inspiring engineering feats that are also aesthetic marvels. The concrete bridge in Bardewadi, Nandi Valley's arch bridge, the Shastri Bridge balanced on fine-looking columns, the bridges of Kankavli and Gokarna, are but a few of the scores of works from the masterful team of Konkan, led by a technocrat at the height of his powers, orchestrating a magnificent opus for generations to cherish.

Welding rails was not a common practice at the time. This was done to reduce the sideways movement of the train and the noise. The Konkan team had seen the use of gas pressure welding technology, but since this was not available in the country, the equipment was imported. Selected skilled workers were sent to Japan for training. The convenience of gas pressure welding was that the welding activity could be done at the construction site itself. Typically, long rails welded at the workshop would be brought to the location of the line. The difficult terrain of the Konkan would not allow this regular procedure. The last but not the least attraction was that welding at the construction site could save two-thirds of the cost of conventional methods.

The Konkan Railway was the first railway organization to use an optic fibre communication network. Sreedharan's decision to lay the most modern optic fibre technology had invited fierce resistance from within the railways. In the nineties, optic fibre was not widely used. Notwithstanding the protests, Sreedharan went ahead with his plan. By now, ironically, the whole of Indian Railways has optic fibre connectivity, but the longest optic fibre network still belongs to Konkan.

Newer technology was also employed in the construction of well foundations to build bridges over rivers, with great success. The bridges across the rivers Zuari and Mandovi, lying close to the sea, required deep piling. Even a regular foundation was constructed in a compressed, air-conditioned environment so that the workers could step into the compressed chambers to dig comfortably. Working 45 metres underground, inside a well, was always going to be a hazardous task. Needless to say, this was also being done for the first time in India.

Yet another challenge was to craft the ventilation systems in the tunnels. As we have seen earlier, at least four of the tunnels along the Konkan line exceeded 3 kilometres in length. Three of them were between 4 kilometres and 6.5 kilometres. It was necessary to have air circulating in all of them. The smoke and dust from the engines that would remain inside the tunnels could harm passengers. The tunnels needed appropriate ventilation to prevent this. But the technology to make that happen was not available in the country. Faced with a task that the railways had never done before, the Konkan team had to find a new solution this time too. Experts were sent abroad to study and explore solutions. They returned to install a world-class ventilation system in the country. Other than DMRC, Konkan was the only institution which possessed the technical knowhow to build tracks in a tunnel with ventilation systems. Their expertise has been put to good use in many other organizations in the country. When Border Roads Organization built a tunnel in Jammu and Kashmir, they relied on the Konkan team to help them implement the ventilation system. The Indian Railways too sought out KRCL for many such projects.

The Konkan mission surged ahead at breakneck speed. But it could only be completed two years later than the original deadline of five years. There was no question of comparing the Konkan with any of its predecessors. If the original plans were executed on schedule, the mission could have been completed much earlier. The delay of two years was on account of the 105-kilometre stretch passing through the state of Goa, where it came up against fierce protests that for some time blocked the mission from building even an inch of line there. Stoppage of work at one of the main arteries of the project had a cascading effect on other sections of the mission. It was a very trying hurdle for Sreedharan and his teammates. It was a great lesson, the tenacity and doggedness with which he and his team toiled on, even as the intense embers of controversies and stalling tactics smouldered about them.

The mission lost nine months, not for any reason relating to technology, but on account of politics. From the vantage point of having seen the outcome of the mission and the benefits it has brought, anyone would agree that the protests and quarrels that stalled it were an exercise in futility. The major sticking point was the agitators' demand to redraw the Konkan Railway's original alignment. There were sinister subplots in their protest, with political, communal and religious special interest groups joining the melee. After the commotion of heated arguments and counter-arguments had died down, the original alignment prepared by KRCL and approved by the Goa government was allowed to be constructed. What was left was the bad aftertaste of the irretrievable loss of invaluable time, and Rs 100 crore of taxpayers' money!

The protests that raged against the Konkan line's alignment came to a flashpoint on 26 March 1993 when the prime minister directed a halt to the project in Goa. The protesters had several demands. The first related to environmental protection, which the alignment was accused of endangering. Another concern was the potential adverse effects of the new tracks on Goan heritage and culture. Yet another was that the alignment would divide the people of Goa. The solution, according to the protesters, was to redraw the alignment avoiding environmentally sensitive areas and farmlands in the state. Another suggestion was to move the alignment eastwards to the foot of the mountains to facilitate future development of the higher regions. An in-depth analysis of the demands and the source of protests reveals many factors at play. The foremost driver was politics. Local politics in Goa was in turmoil, and its relationship with the central government in a stalemate. The imbalanced distribution of power among the religious groups in various regions of Goa, their spheres of influence and the protracted feud among the factions, added to the fire.

Goa had 105 kilometres of the Konkan line. Of that, the 22-kilometre Pernem–Mahim and the 29-kilometre Balli–Loliem segments were not contested. The 55-kilometre portion between Balli and Mahim fetched all the protests. The southern region, known as the granary of Goa, the swamplands of Carambolim Lake, which was a favourite haunt for migratory birds, and the rainforests by the shores of the Zuari and Mandovi rivers, the Cumbarjua canal, Chapora, Talpona, Galji Bagh and Tiracol, and the densely populated areas in Old Goa like Salsit, Madgaon and Quepem were included in the alignment. The 500-year-old St Francis Xavier Church's proximity of 1.5 kilometres to the alignment was hotly protested. As if all this was not bad enough, the special interest groups from real estate business joined the protest party too. The real estate Mafiosi opposed the line fearing that its presence along the shores of Goa would reduce the demand for and price of the precious seafront land.

Crossing the Red Signals in Goa

In 1993, as the controversies around the alignment through Goa raged, two segments of the Konkan rail line had been opened for passenger train operations—the Roha–Dasgaon line, now called the Vir line, and the Mangalore–Udupi line. Local people living along those lines celebrated the inauguration of these lines as their own. V. Anand remembered one of those celebrations, where the Konkan crew had been received with the kind of fanfare accorded to, maybe, astronauts. People waited for the train crew with aarti, garlands, special clothes and sweets. They threw flowers at the crew and rushed to the train to touch it. They wondered aloud whether the trains would really take people from the remote little corners all the way to Bombay and Delhi. Some in the crowd teared up, saying they could not believe a railway through their region could happen in their lifetime. The chief guests at the inauguration in Roha were the Union minister for railways and the chief minister of Maharashtra. The Mangalore–Udupi line was inaugurated in the presence of Prime Minister Narasimha Rao and the Karnataka chief minister.

The struggles in Goa did not impact progress of work on other parts of the Konkan line. But they did raise the spectre of uncertainty about the project as a whole. The environmentalists argued that the wide, 18,000-hectare, traditional paddy fields on the plains along the shores of the Zuari and Mandovi rivers, and their natural fertility, would be destroyed with the arrival of trains in the region. The land acquired for the project had taken away 2000 hectares of paddy fields. The fields, which yielded 40,000 tonnes of rice yearly, depended on the monsoon and the tidal flow of the rivers for their irrigation. The concern that the flow of water across the field would be blocked and cause the soil to lose fertility was an important one. The campaign that spread this story picked up in intensity quite quickly. The interesting fact was that every government in Goa had approved this plan all along. The alignment the railways drew across Mapusa, Panaji, Madgaon and Canacona was approved by the state government in 1988 when Pratap Singh Rana was the chief minister. Other parts of the contested alignment had been sanctioned in 1990 by Dr Luis Barbosa's ministry. Meanwhile, Chief Minister Ravi Naik's government re-examined the alignment. Its committee, which included local representatives, ratified the alignment with minor changes. In 1991, before the Konkan alignment was drawn, Minister for Railways Jaffer Sharief had convened a meeting in Delhi. Sreedharan pointed to the difficulties in changing the alignment in that meeting. If a new alignment had to be worked out, the project, for that reason alone, would be delayed by years, as it would require an additional 19 kilometres of track, including 7.5 kilometres of tunnels. Costs would escalate by Rs 55 crore. And, considering the loss of time that new surveys, studies and approvals would entail, the overheads for the project as a whole could go beyond Rs 250 crore. The ministry sent a memo to the State of Goa, saying that Goa would be responsible for these additional expenses and also for explaining to the other states the reasons for delay of construction of the Goa leg of the Konkan. The Ravi Naik government, upon receiving this memo, decided that the alignment did not have to change, except for minor tweaks to the segment that passed through the densely populated Balli–Madgaon region. The chief minister's letter was sent to the ministry of railways on 30 September 1990. Additionally, the Indian Railways constituted a single-member committee to review the demands and the proposal from Goa in October. The single member was himself a Goan, Manuel Menezes, who had once been chairman of the Railway Board. Additional adjustments suggested in the committee report were added to the alignment. Even after accommodation of all these suggestions, resistance to the project was still on the rise. Sreedharan took a hard-line stance.

He would respond to future crises during the course of project delivery in exactly the same way. His thoughtful views on development projects had always been that suggestions and opinions have value and their rightful place during the planning phase. Developed countries throughout the world follow such an approach. They would take a long time to plan such projects, especially in the case of infrastructure development such as alignments for railway lines. Opinions and suggestions from the public would be solicited at this time. When the final blueprint had been drawn and construction had begun, there would not be any more changes. The project would have to be carried out, whatever the obstacles. Even a minor variation in the plan would cost an unpredictable amount of money and irrecoverable loss of valuable time. Sreedharan's always held that making room for changes would prevent the project from achieving its real goal. Hence, he took the hard-line position on the Konkan project and on all the other projects that followed.

One of the other protests in Goa related to the 72-hectare Carambolim Lake, a source of water for irrigation of the surrounding fields and a sanctuary for migratory birds. The protestors said the area would be at environmental risk if the topography were to change in any way. The coastal state of Goa had been the habitat for about twenty different kinds of water plants. The complaint was that the project would wipe out 197 hectares of those plants, leading to an ecological disaster. Although the line did not go through any forest conservatories, apprehensions were abound on that front too. And there was more, in the shape of rumours that criminals would find it easy to hitch a ride to Goa to add to its crime rate.

Chief Minister Ravi Naik and Transportation Minister Pandurang Raut supported the existing plan. The first salvo from the political front against the alignment came from Edwardo Faleiro, a member of Parliament from South Goa and a minister in the central government. In June 1991, he made a statement that the densely populated coastal regions of Salsit, Quepem and Madgaon would not be able to give up enough land for the project. Instead, he said, the line ought to be moved to the remoter regions. Deputy Chief Minister Wilfred de Souza came forward in support of this argument. The environmental group called Gomantak Lok Paksh and the Christian Church of South Goa too turned out to be major actors in the opposition camp. The protestors rallied under a common banner, 'Konkan Railway realignment action committee'. Making the situation worse, the Hindu communities of north Goa pulled their weight behind the current alignment, which the Christian communities were opposing vehemently. Meanwhile, in April 1992, the action committee filed a petition at the Panaji bench of Bombay High Court. By the end of April, the high court observed that all the arguments opposing the alignment were baseless, and rejected the plea. It also remarked that disagreement over a meagre, 30 hectares of land, to stall the largest railway project in the nation that would benefit the whole country, was not acceptable. Following the ruling, the Government of Goa set up a fifteen-member committee. The committee submitted its report in October 1992. Eight members of the committee voted in favour of an unchanged alignment.

Even with opposition to the alignment mounting pressure on them, the KRCL team did not cow down, but accelerated work everywhere else. Sreedharan was forced to make a statement to the media to explain KRCL's views on the Goan impasse. In May 1992, the corporation issued a press release rebutting, point by point, the arguments against its alignment in Goa. It argued that the current alignment had always been in the best interests of Goa, and if it were to be changed in the manner that the opposing camp wished, the state, instead of losing just 54 hectares of land, would end up losing 350 hectares of precious forest. The statement exposed the protestors' hollow claims.

Sreedharan's media blitz did not directly attack the real instigators of the protests, but his statements drew a vivid picture of the context of, and the reasons behind, the controversies. He also circulated a summary of the several acts of goodwill and the gains for Goa that came from KRCL. He explained that KRCL had acquired only 726 hectares of land, 340 hectares of it farmlands, and 36 hectares of it uninhabited. Twenty-five families were relocated, which was not even close to the protesters' claim that a thousand families would be displaced! All precautions would be taken to keep the traditional practices of cultivation intact. The 7.2 kilometres of the line passing through protected forest land between Balli and Canacona would not be touched, as there would be no construction on it other than a tunnel running underground. Sreedharan made a public promise that the bridges over the Zuari and Mandovi rivers would be done scientifically, based on the latest environmental studies, to leave the ecosystem unharmed. At all stages of developing the plan for Konkan, directions and opinions were sought from the public, directly or through government agencies. The alignment was drawn following the same process, and construction had begun with the documented mandate of stakeholders from all walks of life. Yet, the conflagration in Goa forced the Konkan team to appear before the public to explain itself, Sreedharan recalled.

Every day of delay would mean a loss of approximately Rs 10 lakh to the corporation, and if the alignment were to be redrawn, another Rs 250 crore would have to be spent—KRCL had presented the math to the public and the protestors. Sreedharan continued to get construction works done for the Goa segment until the first quarter of 1992. With KRCL coming out in the open with its views, the two camps, one opposing and the other supporting the alignment, were now openly confronting each other. While the Christian priests' antagonism had turned vociferous, ecology expert Dr Madhav Gadgil publicly denounced the alignment. Dr Gadgil, in an open letter laying out a charge sheet of sorts against the current alignment and KRCL, contended that the question was not so much about the alignment as it was about opting for a plan based on rigorous scientific studies that would guarantee not to harm the environment and the everyday life of the people of Goa. Sensing that the controversy had taken a new turn, KRCL was expecting the central government to intervene at any time. On a Friday,

26 March 1993, what the Konkan Railway had feared did happen. The prime minister's special order arrived at Sreedharan's office, directing construction in Goa to be stopped immediately.

After blocking the project in Goa, the Centre, in June 1993, commissioned Justice Ojha to review the issues. Minister Jaffer Sharief presented the Ojha committee's report in Parliament. It contained recommendations to redress the people's concerns in general. But this report too had concluded that the Konkan Railway's alignment was still the best among the options suggested. However, there were additional suggestions for specific precautions and for provisioning a competent body to oversee the project. Some of the salient suggestions of the report were: creation of a special body to review the ecological impact on the island of Divar from construction of the Zuari bridge and approach roads; protection of historically important churches from possible structural damage caused by the movement of fast trains; provision of irrigation facilities at the granary areas; building of safety fences around the tracks running through densely populated areas; and construction of overbridges for pedestrians.

Following the Ojha committee's report, construction in Goa resumed by the end of 1993. Sreedharan later said the protests had effectively led to a loss of nine months. In other segments of the project, though, significant gains had been made. In March 1993, the 47-kilometre line between Tokur and Udupi opened for operations. In the same month, the first train carrying passengers plied on the

Udupi–Mangalore route. In June, the 47-kilometre Roha–Vir line in Maharashtra was operational too.

There were a few other reasons too for the project's two-year delay. Estimated to cost approximately Rs 2000 crore, the project found it hard to get timely funds, which staggered the construction schedule. The state governments were responsible for one-third of the budget. The rest of the money had to be collected as taxable and non-taxable bonds from the domestic financial market. That was not difficult. But the Harshad Mehta debacle that rocked the stock market in the country thwarted those hopes. The bonds were sold for lesser value than expected. Discounts had to be given on the bonds to attract investors. Accounting for such unexpected setbacks took time and resources, resulting in the delay. Another reason was that Sreedharan himself had to often call off construction works that had been hastily embarked upon without adequate geo-technical studies backing them.

The mission, whose description as a Herculean task would be an understatement, had faced indescribable obstacles along the way. The courage of its engineers, workers and employees to take the challenges head-on took the project past the finish line. They sacrificed a lot, some of them risking their own lives, to pave a path to progress for the generations to come. The hair-raising moments some of the employees and workers toiling on-site faced on their hazardous tasks, make the financial, technological and legal hurdles to the project pale into insignificance. There were those who had to spend months in the middle of the wilderness, cut off from their near and dear, doing potentially fatal tasks without rest or leisure.

On many occasions, totally unexpected and sometimes dangerous situations threw a spanner in the works, especially during tunnel construction in Goa. As we have seen earlier, the tunnels took six years to complete, lending to the delay in the commissioning of the Konkan line. The floods of 1994 in the Mahad region of Maharashtra had become an unforgettable memory for many in the Konkan team. Their vehicles were submerged in the all-consuming mud. Workers had a miserable time at the site. A huge number of labourers and engineers, just inches away from a mudslide—and death—were saved in the nick of time from the top of a mountain in Ukshi on 4 July 1997. There were approximately 200 people at the site. Several vehicles and equipment were buried under the dirt. Hundreds of lives were saved from a giant landslide near Pernem tunnel on 26 August 1997, three months before it could be completed, only because of timely evacuation of workers from the location.

When all 760 kilometres of the line had been executed by May 1998, 265 kilometres had already opened for business. The last-commissioned portions were from Khed to Sharavati; and from Pernem to Goa, a segment that had given many a nightmare to the team, which was completed in 1997. The Udupi–Kundapur line had opened a little earlier.

The mission needed 6 lakh tonnes of cement, 80,000 tonnes of iron, 2 lakh tonnes of structural steel and 1 lakh tonnes of rails. Land acquisition had cost Rs 144.8 crore. Preparation of lands for construction cost Rs 473.15 crore; bridge construction Rs 332.11 crore; tunnels Rs 538 crore; laying of tracks Rs 488.65 crore and railway stations Rs 71.02 crore.

The success of the Konkan mission earned international repute for Sreedharan. Post-independent India had undertaken numerous big-ticket projects in the sectors of rail, roads and irrigation. The Konkan mission had been an incredibly daring one. The media celebrated Sreedharan as nothing short of a superhuman. The construction of the Konkan line had become a textbook model for future projects. Amid all the celebrations, Sreedharan openly acknowledged the freedom he had enjoyed and the authority he was able to wield while in the top post at KRCL, which was a new entity and remarkably different from the railways. There had been several obstacles in his path, created by political and official cliques, and he had had no choice but to take them on. The responsibilities began from finding funds for the mission and stretched to solving everyday issues at the worksites. There was no way he could have achieved anything without the support and trust of his colleagues—this was how Sreedharan viewed the Konkan mission.

The project, dubbed as the pride of the nation, did have its critics. There were a few controversies that indeed had followed, but not before Sreedharan had left the post of CMD at KRCL. The criticism was mostly about the lukewarm financial returns from the Konkan operations, contrary to the great expectations everyone had from the project. The economic viability of the line was actually unquestionable, but the railways' turning its face away from Konkan had a lot to do with the lack of traffic generated by it. That supplementary tracks were not doubled to facilitate better use of the Konkan line was criticized too. The railways did promise doubling of the line, but they reneged on their promise once the Konkan line became a reality. In the face of such criticism, Sreedharan once came forward to defend the value of the Konkan project, and his rebuttal extinguished a lot of the sniping.

Metro Man

His three and a half decades with the Indian Railways and seven years at KRCL ought to have been enough for the nation to remember Sreedharan forever. Having laid the last track of the Konkan line, his thoughts, he admitted, were not much about retirement, even after forty-three years on the tracks. He was already past sixty-five. But, before he had a moment to reflect 'What's next?' he was being celebrated as the chosen one to head DMRC. The task was to implement a modern metro rail system in the country. The new field of work was distinctively different from his earlier missions. Even after the epochal Konkan mission, his identity would be associated with yet another project, for which he would earn the sobriquet of Metro Man, and be known as the father of metro systems in India. The Delhi Metro project came to him quite unexpectedly.

While Sreedharan was winding down after the Konkan mission, plans for the Delhi Metro had acquired momentum. It was probably because of the disastrous Calcutta Metro experience that it took another two and a half decades for the Delhi Metro to be mooted. We have seen that a 16-kilometre stretch of the Calcutta Metro took an indefensibly long twenty-two years to complete, exceeding cost estimates by a factor of fourteen. Although it was the forerunner of mass rapid transit systems (MRTS) in the country and a harbinger of wider possibilities in the future, the lack of timely technology upgrades had established the view that the project had failed to accomplish its goals. Sreedharan, who had played a major role in the project, had evaluated the fiasco and had candidly voiced this opinion. In any case, the lessons from the Calcutta debacle were put to the test in Delhi at the very beginning. The railways too were not itching for another episode of misery. Besides, the regular loss of revenue from suburban train systems discouraged them from planning any new venture. In 1986, the Union ministry for urban affairs took away systems such as the metro from the railways for good. The railways, for their part, only welcomed the move.

The national capital was reeling under rapid population growth, and what with the explosive vehicle growth in the city, it had no choice but to invest in a metro system. Metro systems could work only if the city's population crossed the threshold of ten lakhs. Delhi had crossed that mark in the 1940s itself. In 1950, its population had exceeded twenty lakhs. The city had the dubious distinction of being among the most polluted cities in the world, with the highest density of vehicles in India. Vehicular pollution was estimated to account for two-thirds of the overall pollution in the city's ecosystem.

Any solution to modernize Delhi's public transportation system would have to be rail-based. At least thirty-five studies suggested the same solution. None of them had led to anything concrete. The first such study was carried out in 1957 by the Central Road Research Institute. All the subsequent studies recommended an MRTS for the city. With support from the central government, RITES conducted another study in 1994, recommending a 55.3-kilometre metro network connecting the major hubs of Delhi. It drafted a detailed project report too. The government, led by H.D. Deve Gowda, approved the plan. Japan Bank for International Corporation (JBIC—now JICA) agreed to fund the project. On 3 May 1995, the Union Cabinet gave its approval for the project. DMRC was created, with equal participation from the Government of Delhi and the central government. Of its sixteen directors, five each belonged to the respective governments. Apart from that, the position of chairman of the board went to the central government, and that of managing director to the state government. The managing director would be fully dedicated to DMRC and would be responsible for its everyday operations.

Sreedharan's appointment as the founding managing director of DMRC was as unexpected as it was dramatic. By April 1997, most of the important positions at DMRC had been filled. Assistant Company Secretary P.K. Gupta was the first employee to join the corporation. Saroj Rajwade became its financial adviser, and D.D. Pahuja its chief electrical engineer. The search was on for a candidate to fill the most important position; however, there was no shoo-in candidate in sight for the MD's post, which commanded a wide range of powers and needed someone who possessed profound experience and consummate technical skills. The Japanese company was cross with DMRC for allowing the position to remain vacant for so long. They had lent funds for the project in February, and they warned that if it could not find an MD by the end of October, the lending process would be halted. The situation demanded the immediate appointment of a suitable candidate to the post.

Sreedharan was first associated with the Delhi Metro as a member of the panel entrusted with the task of finding a managing director. This is how the story went: Sreedharan had been recommended for the post at the very beginning. P.V. Jayakrishnan, a senior IAS officer who had been Chief Secretary to the Government of Goa and was later posted in Delhi, had proposed Sreedharan's name. Jayakrishnan had the experience of working with Sreedharan on the Konkan project, and having seen him go about it, was inclined to believe he was the best candidate. Jayakrishnan's colleagues too agreed with the recommendation, but there were certain objections based purely on technical grounds. Sreedharan had retired from the railways seven years ago, at fifty-eight years of age. After retirement, he had worked for the Konkan Railway for another seven years. He was now sixty-five. There was a legal statute blocking anyone of that age from leading an organization that was partly owned by the central government. This provision made it impossible for Sreedharan to be considered for the post. He was instead asked to help with finding a suitable recruit. The panel included Delhi Chief Minister Sahib Singh Verma, Lieutenant Governor Tejendra Khanna and Minister for Transportation Rajendra Gupta. Sreedharan joined them.

The panel met several times to discuss potential candidates without finding a good fit. In the end, the panel decided to call off any further meetings and recommended Sreedharan as the right candidate for the post. There was no question that the organization deserved Sreedharan as its leader. Hunting for a resource outside when he was available and willing to head the corporation would be a gross waste of time. The panel, which had top administrators and bureaucrats, had also recognized that there were legalities that prevented Sreedharan's appointment, and were determined to resolve it. The only condition Sreedharan demanded was complete freedom in delivering the project and selecting his team, which the panel readily agreed to. Now the panel, minus Sreedharan, racked their brains to tackle the age issue. The news had reached the highest level.

The panel had to somehow find a way to appoint Sreedharan to the post. One concern related to the health of the sixty-five-year-old. A group of doctors from the railways was assembled to review Sreedharan's physical fitness. The doctors declared him fully fit for the job. The first hurdle was now crossed. The next was the service rule that laid down an upper age limit for government appointments. The Cabinet Secretary at the time, T.S.R. Subramanian, took a bold decision. On the file that processed the candidature, he wrote, 'If this country could be governed

by a seventy-five-year old, why could not a sixty-five-year-
old Sreedharan run an organization such as DMRC?'
He made a compelling endorsement of Sreedharan's
candidature. The move was quite unprecedented. Before
Sreedharan's appointment, a government servant of that
age had never been appointed in a comparable institution,
and it has not happened since. It was the administration's
trust in Sreedharan's capability that drove them to go the
extra mile to have him at the helm of a new venture.

The year was 1997, and it was already October.
Sreedharan's responsibilities at the Konkan Railway
had come to a fulfilling end. But the period between
4 November and 15 December saw him make back-to-
back trips between Mumbai and Delhi without respite. The
employees hired earlier and the new recruits transplanted
from KRCL helped him run DMRC until a full team was
in place. A.K.P. Unni, who had been officer on special
duty at the Konkan Railway, had moved to DMRC too.

Sreedharan had become a much-loved media favourite,
with many newspaper columns richly praising the incredible
stories that came out of Konkan. In Kerala, of course, the
Malayalee angle was played up a lot. News magazines in
the state devoted reams of newsprint celebrating every
success of the Konkan project that was headed by a native
son of the state. When Sreedharan was appointed to head
DMRC, it was not just the local media, but the national
media too that celebrated the news.

Sreedharan officially took up the new job on
4 November 1997. In the beginning, DMRC did not

even have a building to function out of. Two rooms, one each offered by the Union ministry for urban affairs and Rail Bhavan, were its temporary offices. The room in the ministry's office was occupied by Pahuja, Gupta and Rajwade, while the registered office of the Konkan Railway in Rail Bhavan seated Sreedharan and Unni. Here began the initial legwork for DMRC. Soon, an office was set up in the Pragati Vihar hostel building near Lodhi Road. In the early days, the hostel did not have enough amenities, including electricity and water, to run the shop. Yet, the entire planning for the metro was done according to schedule, despite these inconveniences. To expand the office, three floors of the building were later leased and furnished.

Sreedharan's next effort was to assemble his team. He brought in many skilled personnel from the railways in temporary capacities. Sreedharan personally oversaw the hiring process, interviewing each of the candidates, recruiting them on the basis of his own assessment of their abilities. By the end of 1998, he had recruited close to one hundred employees, all between the ages of eighteen and thirty. Seventy per cent of the experienced hires had come from the railways. The rigour of the selection process attracted some criticism. The slow pace of recruitment was mainly due to the time it took to vet the candidates for all aspects of the requirements, but some read it as a sign of certainty of delays in the project itself. But Sreedharan's lightning moves right after the hiring process ended proved those concerns to be nothing more than speculation.

Although Sreedharan had been pledged non-interference in the running of DMRC, he revealed later that it was not always the case. There were relentless attempts early on to influence appointments, contracts and land acquisitions. At each instance, Sreedharan stuck to his convictions and decisions, regardless of the consequences of not yielding to vested interests.

Ethics and personal integrity for an employee at DMRC were as indispensable as their professional skills if they were to stay on. According to Sreedharan, to be honest at DMRC meant more than the mere meaning of the word. It was not enough to possess professional integrity, employees had to be seen as people with integrity so that everyone could recognize that trait in them instantly. The selection process had been a protracted one for exactly this reason, testing recruits for both honesty and competence. New recruits had to sign a document containing a nine-point code of conduct, declaring their commitment to ethics and moral values. Some of the codes ran thus: do not make illicit profit in the form of cash or otherwise while part of the organization; do not conspire or lobby for personal gains or self-aggrandizement; do not misuse the position for selfish gains; do not indulge in business or trade while being employed; do not indulge in immoral activities such as adultery; do assist in eliminating corruption, etc.

Although the technical personnel at DMRC were recruited from all over the nation, they did not really have adequate knowledge of metro systems. But Sreedharan would not compromise on his expectations from every engineer on his team, unwilling to accept that his or her skills should be anything less than world-class. He kept reminding them that a technician's concerns should not just be about the pay cheque or the benefits, or about the attainment of glory or climbing up the ladder of designations. The only way to gain respect and recognition from peers and supervisors was to acquire the deepest knowledge and skills of one's job, and improve and adapt them to the changing times. Promotions and positions would naturally find them.

The nation had begun its first metro system in Calcutta. But, by the time the Delhi project was planned, metro technology had advanced beyond anyone's wildest imagination. The only way to learn it was by visiting foreign countries where metros of the latest technology had been constructed. The newly hired engineers were divided into two teams comprising twenty members each. These two groups of engineers, including those from the telecommunications, signalling and electrical trades, were sent to eight countries that had metro systems. That was in 1998. One group went to South Asian countries and to Japan. The other group went to Europe. The twenty-day itinerary's sole purpose was to seek and learn all aspects of metro systems. The typical side-pleasures of such sojourns, like shopping, sightseeing, etc. were completely discouraged. In some countries, the touring engineers spent only a few hours. The moment they got down at the airport, they would head straight for the country's metro network and also attempt to study its corporate system, visit its production centres and schedule meetings with the experts in the industry. As soon as their purpose was served, the team would move on to the next destination. For the engineers who had migrated from the railways, this was a novel and refreshing experience. The engineers also trained with foreign consultancies for as long as three to four months. The Delhi Metro's regular international consultancies—Pacific Consultants International (PCI), Parsons Brinckerhoff International (PBI) and Japan Railways Technical Service (JARTS)—provided four-to-five-month training sessions to the engineers. It was a great opportunity for the young engineers at DMRC to be able to learn the latest technologies that were in use in Europe and the United States. These days, India does have training facilities for engineers. In 2002, DMRC instituted a metro technology training centre for engineers at Shastri Park. Professionals on deputation from the railways instruct junior engineers, who are later sent to Hong Kong for another three months of training. The DMRC institute was the only one of its kind in south Asia.

Since the planning and delivery had to be done at an accelerated pace, the administration was lean, just as it had been deliberately kept so at KRCL. The ultimate power being vested with the managing director, the ten-member board of directors did not involve themselves in the everyday activities of DMRC. The conventional management approach was replaced with a modus operandi based on a set of policies that came from Sreedharan's long years of experience, and his wisdom and pragmatism. Each officer had staggering responsibilities, and had to take part in multiple tasks, resolve complex issues and instruct their wards. In each instance, the priority was always quick decision-making. Taking a decision on any issue the same day it arose was strictly enforced. 'Resolution without slacking' was the diktat handed out to the officers, along with the problems they were assigned to solve. The weekly meetings conducted by the department heads reviewed the planning and progress of the project. As in the Konkan case, there were no minutes kept of meetings, even those attended by the top fifty officials of DMRC. They would disassemble after the routine review of the previous week's progress and the setting of the current week's schedules and goals. Every month, there would be another meeting of middle managers. This way, the management could ensure every member's participation in project delivery.

Sreedharan would gift each officer at the executive level a copy of the Bhagavad Gita with Swamy Vidya Prakashananda's interpretation at the time of their recruitment. The Swamy belonged to the Sri Suka Brahma Ashram of Kalahasti in Andhra Pradesh. The gift undoubtedly communicated to its recipients what Sreedharan expected of them, and became an infinite source of motivation at DMRC. Sreedharan did not distribute the Gita to endorse a particular religion in his organization. He cherished the work as the foundational document of management practices with which to run DMRC. There was no better way to convey the message of fulfilling one's karma in order to be beneficial to society, while also finding avenues to refresh oneself. The gift inspired its readers to brush all mounting troubles aside and immerse themselves in their duty. On Mondays, during the meeting of the department heads, the recitation of shlokas and discourse on them was a usual practice. Sreedharan had always believed in and championed the need to inculcate and reinforce such values in people, even during his school days.

The Big Leap

It would be interesting to get a perspective of the giant leap made by metro systems across the world at the time the Delhi Metro was in the works. The metro revolution that began in 1863 with an underground tunnel in London had spread around the world since the early twentieth century. Developed countries had invented newer technologies and implemented metro systems in all their major cities. When the 150th anniversary of the metro was celebrated in London in January 2013, more than 180 cities around the world had by then acquired the metro mode of transportation. Construction had begun on new metros in another fifty cities. Available statistics show approximately 7000 stations and 8000 kilometres of global metro tracks in operation currently. Although the metro system had evolved in Europe, it were the Asian countries, led by Japan, who had made giant strides in metro technology, and had the most advanced tracks. The biggest of all the metros in the world, with the largest number of stations and the longest track, was the New

York City Subway—338 kilometres, with 468 stations. In terms of capacity, it ranks seventh in the world. The metro at Seoul had built a reputation for its cleanliness, modern amenities, and operations that were on schedule. Talking about amenities, there was an eye-popping array of them—automatic platform gates, digital signage at all gates, touchscreens with Google maps, announcements in English and the local language, contactless smart card ticketing, e-money transfer and so on. It was also heavily patronized, standing right behind the Tokyo Metro in terms of passenger traffic. The other heavily used metro systems were those of Beijing and Moscow. The Tokyo Metro had approximately 300 stations and carried 80 lakh commuters every day. The Moscow Metro, operated entirely by the government, carries 70 lakh people every day. It has 312 kilometres of track on twelve lines, with trains plying every minute and a half. Beijing Metro in China stood first in terms of the number of passengers transported daily, its commuters exceeding the one crore mark by March 2013. China became the number one metro country, developing services at a rapid pace. China intended to increase its lines from seventeen to nineteen, and its total track length to 700 kilometres by the year 2015. This was the broad picture of the state and future plans of metro systems worldwide at the time of inception of DMRC.

A general consultant—which eventually turned out to be a consortium of three consultancies—was to be hired to begin planning the metro system in 1998. Six tenders were invited. DMRC reviewed them for financial and technical standards. The consultants who made it to the consortium were PCI, PBI and JARTS. The appointment of PCI as lead consultant in the consortium brought the criticism that there was a conflict of interest in their appointment since they were in-house consultants to JBIC, who were lenders to the Delhi project. The situation was interpreted as DMRC's inability to be transparent in its decisions. The rumour gained ground and could not be sidestepped. The government then decided to review the selection process. DMRC explained their side of the story and revealed the procedures followed in selecting the consulting service provider. It became obvious that there was no foul play and that the appointment was done purely on the basis of merit. With that, the rumours were stilled. A side note on the issue was that a news daily which had been relentlessly publishing stories maligning DMRC later confessed to its mistake and publicly apologized.

Three sections made up the first phase of the project. The first was the 8.3-kilometre Red Line, which would start from Dilshad Garden and end at Rithala. It was also called the east-west bound Shahdara–Tis Hazari line. Most of the track ran along a viaduct 10 metres high above the roads. The construction of this viaduct, which crossed over the Yamuna River between the Shastri Park and Kashmere Gate stations, had to be done while the daily traffic plied below. As the Red Line expanded, and the Tis Hazari–Inderlok, Inderlok–Rithala and Shahdara Dilshad Garden segments were brought into its fold, the line grew to 25.09 kilometres.

The second section—the Yellow Line—had a first phase connecting Vishwa Vidyalaya and Kashmere Gate, which was 11 kilometres long. This was also the first track of the metro that ran through a tunnel. The extended, 44.65-kilometre section had 34 stations between HUDA City Centre of Gurgaon in Haryana and Jahangirpuri in the north. Both ends of the line were designed to run on elevated tracks, while the middle section, which ran through densely populated localities, would use tunnels. The third section—the Blue Line—was also designed to take the metro out of the city. It stretched from Dwarka Sub-City in the west to Noida in the east. Half of it would run on elevated tracks and the other half underground. The 60-kilometre line would cross the Yamuna, connecting Indraprastha and Yamuna Bank station. The hanging bridge above the existing railway bridge was constructed as part of the Blue Line project.

The planning and design could not, of course, materialize without its fair share of disputes. As soon as DMRC came up with a plan for each section, calls for innumerable changes would come from all corners. The Delhi government had demanded many corrections to the plans at every juncture. They were typically driven by backroom pressure groups to do so. DMRC made several presentations to the central government. As suggestions and recommendations continued to be reviewed and adapted, time flew. Many observers, justifiably, had the strong impression that the Delhi Metro could not be anything much more than a paper project!

Meanwhile, DMRC made an important, strategic move. They began the construction of the Shahdara–Tis Hazari line, which did not invite too many requests for changes, in double quick time. The campaign against DMRC, that it was just another 'white elephant' in the making, had already been doing the rounds. DMRC plunged full throttle into action, conducting detailed surveys of the Shahdara–Tis Hazari section, issuing invitations for tenders and land acquisitions to blunt such apprehensions. Work to reinstall the disturbed infrastructure in the area, such as water pipes, electricity and telephone lines, was underway. The local traffic routes too were realigned. Efforts to coordinate and communicate with the public had already begun much earlier. Apart from the officials at DMRC, officials from the police, the water authority and other government office representatives had taken part in DMRC's open forums to interact with the general public. The process helped DMRC gain an early understanding of the difficulties and complaints of the public when the project moved into the implementation phase. There were about 500 such programmes for direct interface with the affected population. The problems they eventually faced on account of the construction were relatively minor, and might have been easily resolved even without these meetings. But there was always the possibility that even a small problem ignored early on might fester into chaos and escalate into a major crisis. This had to be prevented.

DMRC proactively dealt with complaints about blocked entryways, breached fences, broken water pipes, snapped electric lines, etc. The corporation would facilitate redressal of complaints by guiding the complainants or even pooling money from the project's budget to help them out. All this made for a refreshing experience to the people of Delhi. Until then, no development project in the area had ever consulted, or even considered, the city dwellers' concerns or discomfort.

The first phase of the project did not really need much private land. Yet, Sreedharan took the same approach he did at Konkan. Instead of taking legal recourse as a first step, DMRC officials met with the land or house owners directly to inquire about their needs. They let them know that the alignment would not change, but that the owners were entitled to appropriate compensation or rehabilitation in order to facilitate vacation of the earmarked locations as soon as possible. It was important to note that the Government of Delhi supported DMRC to the hilt in staying the course on the final draft of the alignment. The final portion of the alignment had to go through a block of buildings holding a cluster of lawyers' offices at Tis Hazari. The lawyers put up a voluble resistance, blocking the land acquisition programme and noisily demanding to meet Chief Minister Sheila Dikshit. She, however, would only reiterate DMRC's stand that the alignment would not change. It had been drafted after many months' deliberations, and it was not prudent to change it even as work on it progressed. However, the government had given assurances to the agitators that the construction would not interfere with their activities or business in any way. This assurance yielded the desired results.

The presence of various religious places in the project area posed a major headache. DMRC relocated many places of worship using its own funds. During the time of construction at Shahdara, DMRC moved a temple and its deity to Delhi, even constructing a brand new abode for the idols. Shahdara also had around 300 small business owners who were dislocated. They were rehabilitated in shops constructed for the purpose, and not too far away from their original location. Although the government was responsible for taking these measures, DMRC stepped in, realizing the government's lackadaisical business-as-usual attitude, and themselves reached out to the traders to arrive at amicable settlements.

When the Shahdara–Tis Hazari line was in progress, the funds pledged by the Japanese lender had not been disbursed. The funding plan was to get the state and central governments to cover 15 per cent of the project cost each, with the Japanese lender providing the bulk of the investment—about 60 per cent. The remainder of funds had to be earned by developing supplementary business centres and from advertisement revenues. The cost of delay would be Rs 2.3 crore per day. In between, there were doubts concerning the loan from Japan, as the international political reaction to the Indian nuclear tests in Pokhran was one of disapproval. Sreedharan, who had the ultimate say on financial decisions for the project, went ahead with his schedule to begin the construction phase on the strength of his gut instinct that the loan from Japan would come through. That was indeed a very bold step, but by now such acts of daring decisiveness had become one of his defining characteristics. He stuck to his policy of taking the rigorous decision at the right time. It did not matter if it was right or wrong; it was more important to be able to make a decision. Many a time, Sreedharan would thrust his nose into highly complex situations faced by his deputies to help them make timely decisions. During the development of the Shahdara–Tis Hazari line, a visit Sreedharan paid to the worksite saved DMRC a few crores of rupees. The initial plan was to build a vaulted track between Shahdara and Seelampur. When Sreedharan visited the site, he found that a better and much cheaper alternative would be to pave over an embankment for the track. DMRC's calculations later showed that the decision to abandon construction of the vaulted track had saved it crores of rupees.

Regardless of how large the value of the contract, the tender processes, selection of contractors, and award of contracts were within the powers of the managing director. This had helped get activities going at the quickest possible pace. There were instances of some of the most important contracts being awarded at a turnaround time of just three weeks. Sreedharan would review all high-value contracts, make a swift decision and present the details to the board. Not even once had his decisions been called into question or doubted. Like all other public sector enterprises, public scrutiny and routine audits were applicable to DMRC as well. The corporation was legally subject to review by the Comptroller and Auditor General (CAG), the Central Vigilance Commission (CVC) and Parliamentary committees.

Ushering in a novel scheme such as the metro would, naturally, attract all kinds of obstructive shenanigans. The legal department, which had worked on the project from the very early stages, was able to handle them expertly and render an environment conducive for smooth implementation of the project. Hundreds of legal issues related to land acquisitions, employment disputes tax troubles and contract disputes had already accumulated in the courts. The legal department constituted to manage them had successfully won many cases in favour of DMRC. Sreedharan had given his utmost attention to the legal proceedings. He kept himself informed about the status of all important cases. He was perpetually worried about the potential loss of time and money that may result from legal tangles and unfavourable court rulings.

The proactive support given to the project by the Delhi media had, in a big way, helped it succeed. DMRC consciously built a rapport with the media, maintaining it throughout the duration of construction, and had created an energetic and motivated public relations team at the very start for this purpose. At every point during the project construction, there were instances that could have turned the tide of public opinion turn against DMRC. When tragedies struck, leading to death on some occasions, the media did not respond with negativity. To build goodwill for the project among the citizens, the public relations department devised several programmes, including the staging of street plays.

DMRC did face numerous incidents that left a bad taste in the mouth. The engineer and his colleagues arriving on-site for a land acquisition process would often face an unruly mob hollering death threats and hurling stones at them. Once, a mob manhandled a DMRC team at Khyber Pass—the engineer and the employees were locked up in a room, under threat of being burnt to death. The angry mob's demand was to move the alignment away from their land. Daljit Singh, who would later become deputy chief engineer (land), once walked into a rain of sharp rocks that were hurled at him. Similar experiences had visited DMRC engineers and other employees at Chor Bazaar, Tilak Nagar and Boulevard Road. There were many such episodes. The countless legal troubles, obstructive tactics by recalcitrant bureaucratic and political groups, and the technical snafus were par for the course.

Within two years, work on the second line of the first phase had begun. The 13.7-kilometre underground tunnel was on this line. Tunnel tracks cost more than elevated tracks. But DMRC preferred the former, as it did not disrupt commuters or impact other routine activities in the national capital. The first two phases of the metro consisted of 48.06 kilometres of underground tunnels and 31 stations. The third phase had 41.044 kilometres of tunnels and 28 stations. The tracks that passed entirely through the tunnel under the Chor Bazaar area had to be built at a depth of 25 metres. Construction of another tunnel at Nai Sarak in Old Delhi ran into a little trouble. But timely interventions ensured that the problems were snuffed out. The contractors had employed conventional techniques to build the tunnel here. They had stopped work several times when the machinery got damaged by the huge rock formations underground, and this was causing delays. Even after multiple extensions were given them, the contractors could not finish the task. In the end, DMRC stepped in, instructed them to use a modern technology that the Australians had used to build tunnels. This ensured the completion of the tunnel at Chor Bazar without endangering the historical structures from the Mughal era in the area.

Build activities in the city of Delhi were extremely difficult. Besides the regular deluge of everyday traffic, there were buildings that were set very close, and the crisscrossing roads, water pipes, electric and cable lines made for a snarl of trouble, tripping up the engineers every step of the way. Topping all this were the obstructions and agitations by a stream of disgruntled individuals and organizations who went to court against the project. There were approximately 400 cases filed against the alignment itself, and these litigations came to an end only after the Delhi Metro Railway (Operations and Maintenance) Act was passed in 2002 to curb them. The law granted powers to DMRC enabling it to overstep obstructive actions by local administrative offices, and restrained the lower courts from handing down rulings unfavourable to DMRC. Around 30,000 trees in the city had to be cut down to make way for the tracks. DMRC determined to plan ten trees for every tree felled for the project. They earnestly made sure the plan was followed through. Yet, local government offices obstructed the progress of work citing destruction of trees whose felling was unavoidable. To cut a single tree, DMRC had to make endless trips to many government offices. Each inch of progress meant that an incredible number of approval documents had to be 'passed' by countless government agencies. The list of some of the agencies which were vested with the powers to grant these approvals were the Urban Art Commission, the Central Vista Commission, the Delhi Development Authority, the New Delhi Municipal Council, the Municipal Corporation, the Archaeological Survey of India, the Forest Department, the Fire Department, Mahanagar Telephone Nigam, the Delhi Water Board, BSES and NDPL (Electricity).

The policy of empathy and leniency towards contractors adopted at KRCL was followed in Delhi too. In return, they remained loyal to DMRC's objective of finishing the project on schedule. In fact, the contractors were treated as equal partners in the project. Clearing their bills on time was always the emphasis. The finance department would process their bills within three to four days of their receipt. Should there be any query on a particular item in the bill, contractors were still expected to be paid in full minus the item in question, pending satisfactory explanation. It was mandatory for every dispute to be resolved within a week. The conscious effort to clear bills on time would not only avert unnecessary delays due to lack of funds, but Sreedharan was convinced that tardy payments to those who deserved to be paid on time would lead to corruption and unsavoury relationships and deals. It was not in order at all for the contractors on the project to pay anything out of their pocket. For this reason, the top management always inquired of contractors about the bills due to them. A healthy relationship was maintained between the departments of finance and operations. The high-ranking officers from the finance department were invited to even those meetings where the agenda was mostly technical. This way, the finance experts were able to get a grasp of the real picture and the state of the project, while keeping a fair eye on its financial constraints too.

It is instructive to note that the kind of troubles that occurred in Calcutta never happened in Delhi. Sreedharan was extremely cautious about not repeating the mistakes of the past. When a road was blocked for the arduous task of building the tracks, the team made sure an alternative road was opened for traffic. Ten trees were planted in place of every tree removed. Having spared the water pipes and electric lines at the worksite, the project gained a significant degree of confidence among the people of the city. The dust and mud spilled around the work site were washed away at the end of every day's labour. Brand new techniques and equipment were employed. The Delhi Metro would have likely become a reality even without any of these measures. The conventional notion had always been that development projects of a grand scale were handouts from the government, and that the public was expected to take the strain and inconvenience in their stride. But the Delhi Metro was not another exercise in alienation of the public, wilfully taking advantage of their expectation of distress from every government project. So, although the project might have happened even without all these efforts, Sreedharan's conscientious insistence on making the common man part of the grand scheme and giving him a clear vision of the ultimate benefits that would come his way made all the difference. However, none of this was accomplished the easy way, as a brief survey of the project's timeline reveals.

When the first phase of the mission began, the reverse clocks last seen during the Konkan project appeared at the DMRC office too, set on tables belonging to all the stakeholders and also fixed at all the worksites. Reverse clocks immediately brought in a sense of purpose, inspiration and motivation for the determined march towards the goal of breasting the finishing line on schedule. As always, the project plan displayed a slightly shorter timespan than was really so for completion of tasks. To monitor progress and to organize the planned tasks, a software application called Primavera Project Planner 3.0 was used. The American software company Primavera provided the software through their Indian partner, KGL. This software provided rigorous and valuable information on the overall and point-in-time status of the project, and on the pre-plans and schedules for upcoming tasks, to avoid delays and loss of money. It also held the supply chain data for the project. This system, which monitored and warned of loss of time and money should the project be blocked for any reason, greatly aided project planning. It set the project going like a well-oiled machine, advancing steadily and decisively.

PPP and Some Squabbles

Sreedharan took on the persona of a superman as news of the engineering marvel he had wrought made waves across the nation. The organizational values and work culture at DMRC, which rivalled those at successful private firms, became a talking point even on international forums. Management institutions overseas had adopted Sreedharan's version of a functioning management into their curricula. The public and media took note of not only Sreedharan's unique style of operating efficiently, but also the routines he had established. This was happening in a country whose history of basic infrastructure projects was inextricably entwined with stories of corruption. Sreedharan's style was never about lording it over everyone and dishing out commands. Even his simple personal routines told of his unique way of functioning. His usual arrival at office was between 8.30 a.m. and 8.45 a.m. Office time would always be entirely dedicated to official duty. There would be meetings to attend, which Sreedharan would ensure started on time. His time at the office would be up between 5.30 p.m. and 6.30 p.m. DMRC follows the same routine even today. The eight hours at office, according to Sreedharan, were enough to get through the workday successfully if one did not spend time running personal errands. During implementation time at the metro, nobody took leave of absence for relatively minor health reasons like fevers, colds or headaches. Everyone took care not to take more than two days off at a stretch, even for the death of a relative. Sreedharan would pay a visit to the construction sites on Saturdays to examine the in-progress work in person, and to redress any issues at the location. The emphasis being identification and resolution of problems, the engineers and other workers knew that his visits were never supervisions to be apprehensive about, but a much-awaited and valued occasion to get Sreedharan to take part in their teamwork. His presence on-site imbued his colleagues and workers with a cooperative spirit.

In the early days at DMRC, Sreedharan had little time for anything other than the metro project. He gradually began to find time for spiritual activities from 2003 onwards. Although he used to be a regular reader of the Upanishads and the Gita, a chance participation in Swami Bhoomananda Tirtha's jnana yagya in Delhi became a turning point. It became routine for him and his wife to attend the Swami's discourses whenever he was in Delhi. As he learned more of the Gita, the Yoga Vasishta, the Ramayan, the legends from the Puranas and the Upanishads from the Swami, he felt increasingly inspired. Even after his relocation to Kerala, he continued to visit the Swami's ashram in town and routinely heard his talks on television.

As the first phase of the metro progressed, a drummed-up controversy threatened to shake the very foundation of the mission. It grew to a point where Sreedharan was forced to rethink his involvement with the project. The dispute between the Railway Board on the one side and DMRC, along with the Delhi government, on the other raged, with no consensus in sight for more than a year and a half. The point of contention was choice of gauge for the metro. In the end, disregarding Sreedharan's pleas, the board and the central government's choice was imposed on the team. But it did not take long for the decision to be revealed as an ill-advised mistake.

As part of the Indian Railways' policy, its entire network in India had been using broad gauge. Sreedharan contended that metros all over the world used standard gauge, and that had to be the choice in Delhi too. While the metro was in the works, the quarrel rose to a boil. The railways had its own reasons to reject the idea of a separate gauge exclusively for the metro. Their first line of attack was that Sreedharan's demand was directly in conflict with the railways' policy. There was no need for gauge changes for short-term services such as the metro. If both distance lines and short-term services had the same gauge, the metro could use both networks. Broad gauge, as the name suggested, was broader than standard gauge, and safer. The project report did say that the track would be broad gauge. When the railways had approved the report, Sreedharan was the member engineering on the board, and had signed the report without a word. Only after he became MD at DMRC did he call the railways' attention to the issue, which the Railway Board reviewed again, to conclude that the matter was done and dusted already.

Sreedharan's view was borne out of his desire that metro technology in India stay in tune with the technology in vogue across the entire world. Metro technology across the globe was evolving almost every day. If we were to keep ourselves abreast of the latest developments in the industry, we had no choice but to follow contemporary designs and technology, held Sreedharan. The metros worldwide ran on standard gauge. If we went ahead with broad gauge tracks, the trains that we would import for the metro would have to be retrofitted to operate on broad gauge tracks, guaranteeing a waste of precious time and money. Sreedharan demanded that the railways make an appropriate and sensible decision. When the dispute got out of control, the Union Cabinet intervened, constituting a ministerial committee headed by Home Minister L.K. Advani to study the issue. Most likely under the influence of the Railway Board, the committee of top ministers decided in favour of broad gauge for the metro.

The day the ministers' decision was announced, Sreedharan prepared to resign. However, the Lieutenant Governor of Delhi, Vijay Kapur, got him to stay with the project. Sreedharan could not say no to him. He later thought aloud that it would not be his place to make such choices, and his task was merely to complete the mission assigned to him, which happens to be Delhi's marquee project. As soon as the ministerial diktat came, Delhi Chief Minister Sheila Dikshit, wrote to Prime Minister A.B. Vajpayee asking him to reconsider the decision. The letter took the Railway Board to task for their stubborn stance. The chief minister made it clear that the Railway Board had no role in a project being done by the central and state governments; they, in fact, had exposed their own ignorance on standard gauge, and the metro in Delhi could do very well without the meaningless security certificate from the railways! Even that did not convince the prime minister to reconsider the issue. To quell further argument on the matter, Chairman R.N. Malhotra declared that the board and the central government had made up their minds, and that the issue was considered closed. In 2001, when the Central Empowered Committee of Secretaries met, DMRC placed its appeal in front of them. They too overlooked it. The ministry of railways issued a press release making it loud and clear that the matter would not be discussed ever again. The press release essentially claimed that DMRC's—and, by extension, Sreedharan's—arguments had no substance, and that the Railway Board had made the right decision in the best interest of the people and the nation.

The first phase of the metro was on broad gauge from start to finish. DMRC worked hard to avoid any delays on account of the choice of broad gauge. Right after the Cabinet's verdict, a team of highly skilled engineers hopped on a plane to Rotem Company in South Korea, which was contracted to deliver the trains for the metro. The engineers made a request for a redesign of the trains originally built for standard gauge to fit to broad gauge dimensions. The group had to remain with the company for about four months.

In the end, the gauge dispute was not allowed to slow the pace of progress of the first phase. Sreedharan described how the team took the setback in their stride and continued their work. However, by the time the second phase was about to begin, the central government and the Railway Board had changed their views and their earlier hard-nosed position. They now saw merit in Sreedharan's judgement. As a result, phase two of the Delhi Metro was in standard gauge on the Inderlok–Mundka and Central Secretariat–Badarpur lines. The Airport Metro in its entirety was done in standard gauge. In March 2009, the first train from the Rotem Company built specifically for standard gauge was brought to Delhi. The third phase too was completely done in standard gauge. Sreedharan had later commented that the decision to go with broad gauge was the most severe blow he had endured in his entire career spanning half a century. The resilience and hard work DMRC had put in to annul the adverse outcomes from that poor decision was the only saving grace that prevented what could have been an unjustifiable loss of time and resources. Time itself proved that standard gauge was the right choice for future metros elsewhere in the country. The new metros being built in Bengaluru, Chennai and Kochi would all be in standard gauge.

The modern metro in Delhi was built utilizing the best available technologies from around the globe. DMRC was given ten years to complete all the lines. But the corporation gave itself only seven years to complete the project, declaring it the corporate goal. As a result of this, the first phase was delivered in 2002, with Prime Minister A.B. Vajpayee inaugurating it on 24 December. The first train on a modern metro track in the country rolled out, transporting the prime minister, having cut across every obstacle on the way, overcoming even the operation of Murphy's Law, which usually plays out in projects of this scale. The reference to Murphy's Law has been added in the context of a situation which occurred when the inauguration faced an unexpected snag, and the preparedness of DMRC that saved the day. Before the inaugural train started from Rithala, DMRC had inspected everything, providing for every eventuality they could think of to ensure a smooth opening ride. Everything seemed perfect. The electric lines and sources were tested again and again. Should there be a hiccup in electricity supply from the substation, there was going to be a backup. Everything was ready. At least one person on the team must have thought this to himself: there is, after all, the Murphy's Law of excuses that thwarts human excellence and the most diligently prepared mind. The train had been occupied by passengers, including the prime minister. The inaugural ride began at 10.20 a.m. The moment the train began to roll, the electric connection was lost. The backup line was immediately connected, and even before the travellers could notice anything, the ride resumed. DMRC called the incident a failure of Murphy's Law.

The first phase was finished, with the construction of the Dwarka–Barakhamba corridor of the Blue Line in October 2006. This phase consisted of three segments, and required Rs 10,000 crore in funds. With 59 stations, and a length of 65.11 kilometres, 13.01 kilometres through tunnels and 52.10 kilometres on elevated tracks, this phase, which was estimated to take ten years to build, took DMRC only seven years and three months to complete.

The second phase, whose deadline was set so that it would be ready before the Commonwealth Games, included the Green, Violet and Airport Express Lines, of a cumulative length of 124.63 kilometres, with seventy-nine stations. The first segment of the Green Line comprised the Inderlok–Mundka and Kirti Nagar–Ashok Park lines, and was completed in June 2008. The second phase had, in fact, recorded the fastest turnaround time of four and a half years. When the second phase was completed in August 2011, the Delhi Metro still had to expand by another 190 kilometres. The Tokyo Metro, considered to be the best in the world, was only 2 kilometres longer than the Delhi Metro, whose overall track length will cross 400 kilometres by 2021.

An important event from the second phase was the accident in Zamrudpur that forced Sreedharan to resign. The accident occurred at the construction site on a Sunday morning on 12 July 2009, and put DMRC, which until then had an almost clear accident record for eleven years, under tremendous strain because of the scale of the tragedy and suggestions of negligence on its part. Close to a hundred workers had lost their lives at various sites during the first and second phases of the project. None of their deaths was a consequence of any major accident. What could be termed as a major accident had happened in Laxmi Nagar in 2008, when two lives were lost. However, the tragedy at Zamrudpur was too grave to not require explanation. The gigantic launchers shook the whole region as they fell flat on the site underneath, snuffing out seven lives instantly. The national media relayed the tragic news across the nation. DMRC swung into action immediately and addressed the press at length to provide any details called for to allay people's fears about the project. DMRC was of the view that the media acted responsibly, reporting objectively and without bias on the tragedy.

The same day, Sreedharan, at a press meet called at the DMRC office, announced his resignation from the post of managing director in front of a huge contingent of the press representing almost all the media houses in Delhi. He revealed that his letter of resignation had already been sent to the Delhi chief minister. He had accepted moral responsibility for the accident and the loss of lives. The accident at Laxmi Nagar a year earlier had prompted the implementation of rigorous safety measures and strict supervisions for the project. An independent agency had been contracted for the job. A repeat accident had now dented the confidence of the people in DMRC, Sreedharan pointed out. Given the circumstances, accepting responsibility and resigning from his post was the appropriate thing to do.

It did not take long to find out that a fissure in one of the concrete pillars built for the metro in Zamrudpur had triggered the mishap. Sreedharan had, in fact, come to know about the fissure in March, and had given specific instructions for its inspection to determine its safety. But the expert engineers had advised him that the fissure was superficial and was not in any danger of causing a cave-in. Sreedharan was not happy with the answer. He suggested another round of tests subjecting the pillar to full weight from the top. Clearly, his instructions had not been followed. When a 500-tonne girder had been raised to the top of the pillar, Sreedharan had again instructed the workers to haul it down and take appropriate steps to rectify the damage. Since his instructions had not been followed through, and that was the obvious explanation for the accident, the responsibility solely rested on him and he was ready to resign, recalled Sreedharan.

His resignation caused instant uproar. He was under huge pressure to stay on with the project, the exhortations to him to stay coming from Chief Minister Sheila Dikshit, Union minister for urban development, Jaipal Reddy, and even Rahul Gandhi. He had to be with the project at least till the end of the second phase, the last segment of which was the Airport Express Line, they pleaded. Ultimately, Sreedharan relented to their persuasion. In Sreedharan's own family, the reaction to his resignation was mixed. Immediately after he had announced it, he withdrew to his office, where he received a call from Radha, to whom he explained the unfortunate situation. She too insisted that Sreedharan could not leave the project midway and had to continue the work he had been doing until it was finished. His children, on the other hand, backed Sreedharan's decision, and suggested that he now needed the well-deserved comfort of a retired life.

Sreedharan had always opposed the private-public participation (PPP) route for metro projects. The Delhi Metro's Airport Express Line was the first PPP metro line in the country. Reliance Infra, a well-known private company, worked with DMRC as a PPP partner in constructing and operating the 22.7-kilometre Airport Express Line. Sreedharan's views on the PPP model were proved right. It did not take long for the deal to turn sour.

Reliance Infra joined DMRC as a partner for the second phase of the Delhi Metro, to construct and operate the high-speed rail corridor for the Airport Express Line. Apart from providing technical support, DMRC built the tracks for the line too. Reliance Infra was given rights to operate the line that connected the New Delhi airport with the hubs in the city. The line began functioning from February 2011. Soon, the company and DMRC could not see eye to eye, and stumbled into such bitter disagreements that operations were shut down within a year of their start. The shutdown was enforced on 7 July 2011. Contractually, Reliance Infra had taken over the project for thirty years. The company said they had taken the extreme step because of the heavy financial losses incurred on expensive repairs and the high cost of general maintenance. Sreedharan let Reliance Infra know that if they would not honour the contract and resume operations immediately, there would be consequences such as fines and a likelihood of DMRC taking over the operations from them. 'Reliance Infra could not finish the tracks on schedule. The line, originally expected to be operational before the Commonwealth Games began, took another five months to complete. Even then they could not run the trains at the desired speeds. They did not even seem to make an effort to improve performance or efficiency. The trains too did not measure up to DMRC standards,' said Sreedharan. DMRC rejected Reliance Infra's attempts to wriggle out of the contract. As all means of escape were closed to them, Reliance Infra was forced to reopen the line. The line opened on 22 January 2003, but performance still fell short of the requirements in the contract. The trains ran at much lower speeds than stipulated. That resulted in a drop in passenger traffic on the line, which used to have a healthy number of patrons though tickets were relatively pricey. The people could see that while the other metro lines performed admirably, the PPP experiment for the metro, which had fuelled high hopes, had fallen apart spectacularly, appearing to justify Sreedharan's concerns about it.

Sreedharan had always been quite candid about his views on the viability of private participation in public transportation projects like the metro. As the patriarch of metro projects in the country, Sreedharan's unyielding stand had often led to controversy and heated debate.

He stood by his position that the government should underwrite projects that required thousands of crores of rupees in investment. In the short term, he said, these projects, typically, would not be able to make any profits. To incentivize private investors, governments would be forced to give away huge discounts. Investors usually expect access to and ownership of key public real estate, as well as tax reductions in lieu of immediate returns on investments. This would be detrimental in the long term, as the government's revenue sources would be depleted in the bargain. Metros are expected to operate in the public space and had to be within reach of the common man in terms of affordability. Profit-based companies would not be able to operate in this sector without jacking up commuter tariffs. Sreedharan wrote to Planning Commission Vice Chairman Montek Singh Ahluwalia explaining his arguments against PPP in 2008. Later, in his capacity as head of the action committee for urban transportation and planning, Sreedharan let the central government know his views in writing. He called their attention to the fact that 90 per cent of metros around the world were operating under public ownership. The PPP projects in the cities of London, Bangkok and Malaysia had failed. Citing several examples, he proved that nowhere in the world had a privately owned metro company ever run successfully.

There was already a furore over the Hyderabad Metro, announced as the largest PPP metro project in the country. The unsavoury climax of the dispute once again highlighted Sreedharan's thoughtful perspective on the issue. DMRC was appointed as consultant to build a 771-kilometre metro in Hyderabad, staggered over six phases. At an expected investment of Rs 12,132 crore, construction and operation of the first phase, which was to be finished in 2014, was contracted to Maytas Infra, a sister concern of the Satyam group of companies. Sreedharan realized that the project modelled on the PPP concept, which had been flagged off with inordinate fanfare, was running off track from the very word go. He openly criticized the programme as lacking in transparency, as one that was nothing more than a conduit to siphon off public wealth, and which would bring no benefits to the common man. His critique hit home—the impact was unprecedented.

The leadership of the central and state governments launched a counterattack on Sreedharan and DMRC. All this happened just a month and a half after Maytas Infra had signed the contract. The concerned government authorities threatened legal action against Sreedharan for his 'outburst', unless he apologized for it.

Sreedharan's charges against Maytas Infra were hard-hitting. Their pressure tactics on DMRC to redraw the planned alignment, and their attempts to include certain areas in the metro footprint against conventional wisdom, bared their true motivation, at the heart of which lay real estate business interests. Maytas's unexplained rejection of government grants came under the scanner. Sreedharan wrote to the Planning Commission asserting that the proposal of transferring 300 acres of government land for the project would be a recipe for another corruption scandal. As the controversy raged, with back-and-forths both opposing and supporting Sreedharan's stand, the country was jolted into reality by the breaking news of financial scams by Ramalinga Raju's Satyam group. The real face of the Satyam group, which had been cooking the books to skim thousands of crores of rupees in illegal gains for itself, was revealed to the country. The country did not need to know much more to imagine what Maytas's real objectives in taking up the Hyderabad project must have been! The government swallowed their criticism of Sreedharan as they cancelled the contract with Maytas in 2009. Currently, the project is underway on the basis of another contract with L&T, at a much higher price tag. The lingering worry that the price tags may result in higher tariffs, compared with the Delhi Metro rates, remains.

Rejecting Sreedharan's scathing criticism, the central government eventually did draw up a policy favouring the PPP model. Kamal Nath, the Union minister for urban development, announced the government policy in 2013, making it clear that all new metro projects in the country would adopt the PPP model. He said 18 per cent of all metros worldwide were being built and operated on this model, and it would be given due emphasis in India too.

Delivering the Dream

'A gratifying finish to a fifty-year-long career,' remarked Sreedharan, as he bid adieu to DMRC. Since his first job in 1954 at the port of Bombay and until this time, he had lived the official life for forty-seven years, fourteen of them as MD of DMRC. Having successfully delivered the first and second phases of the Delhi Metro, he stepped down on 31 December 2011. He had left behind in the capital a world-class metro system, administering a new work culture, placing the organization on the rails as a thriving enterprise. He was now handing over the reins to capable hands and walking out the door.

At the time of Sreedharan's retirement, the Delhi Metro was transporting 22 lakh passengers every day. In other words, the metro had replaced at least one lakh vehicles on the road, saving the burning of approximately one lakh tonnes of fuel every year (as of 2011). In addition to saving precious petrodollars, the metro had curbed the increase in air pollution, in which matter Delhi was at a dangerous precipice. Studies revealed that the arrival of the metro had in fact cut air pollution by 27 lakh tonnes per year, and the road accident rate by at least 500 city residents a year. Every time a commuter opted for the metro, he or she would be saving twenty-eight minutes of the day from a single ride. Return journeys would save the traveller at least fifty-six minutes. If we were to convert the net profit yielded by the time saved into labour-hours, 20 lakh hours would be the savings—in other words, surplus human labour of 2.5 lakh hours every day. Delhi could make use of the surplus time available to its people to build a brighter future for itself.

The metro's role in transforming the culture of the city commute in Delhi has been phenomenal. The media took note of and highlighted the civil behaviour of metro employees or passengers, which was in stark contrast to that in most other public spaces in the cities of the region, where road rage and criminal assaults on fellow citizens were very common. The regular spectacle of filth and squalor around the major railway stations in Delhi could not be found anywhere on the metro. It would be interesting to note that the railways and metro lines lay just a ten-minute distance apart. Both are used by the inhabitants of the same city. The usual abomination of spit-stained walls at the stations of the Indian Railways or the piles of trash on their platforms were not sights to be associated with the metro. It is a great example of a confident, self-respecting and high-class service inspiring a culture of civility in its patrons.

The Delhi Metro's financials have been sound from the outset. It very quickly became one of the only five profitable metros of the roughly 200 metros operating around the world. By the time he stepped down, Sreedharan had made sure the metro was able to break even as soon as it possibly could and was poised to make profits as well. The metro had been built through tunnels and scaffoldings hoisted on pillars. Minimizing the tunnels helped ease budgetary strains, encourage investments and bring profitability. Twenty per cent of the daily revenue was diverted to ancillary development, adding to the income. Limiting the number of employees, to match international standards in manpower without compromising on efficiency, added to DMRC's strong performance.

The success of the Delhi Metro has been the main motivating force behind the clamour for metros from all large cities in India. Following Delhi, eight more cities have begun work on metros. Bengaluru, Chennai, Mumbai, Hyderabad, Jaipur, Kochi and Kolkata (for a second line) have embarked on metros of their own. Yet another clutch of cities such as Pune, Lucknow, Ahmedabad and Kanpur have begun planning metros. DMRC has helped plan and coordinate construction work for all the metros that have been flagged off so far. It led the projects from the front—right from the survey stage to pre-planning studies and preparation of detailed project reports. They advised project teams, beginning with briefing them on the complex process of obtaining approvals from disparate government authorities. DMRC had been ad hoc consultants for some projects, and primary consultants with some other projects. Sreedharan observed that the driving force behind

DMRC's taking on additional responsibilities had been no more than a call to serve, having been the harbinger of and catalyst for the metro revolution that took the public transportation system in India by storm.

Sreedharan was effusive in his praise for DMRC. At a ceremony where he was awarded by the All India Management Association for excellence in management, he said, 'DMRC is a government enterprise. It adheres to all norms and procedures laid down by the government. So it's like any other government organization. It comes under the supervision of the Comptroller and Auditor General, the Vigilance Commission, the Parliamentary committee and the legislative committee. That DMRC achieved success despite restrictions had dumbfounded many. We'd completed the first phase earlier by two years. The second phase was done with six months to spare. How we were able to accomplish those within the constraints of time and budget ought to be the subject of academic studies. IIM Ahmedabad had joined Oxford University to do a study on DMRC. Managements from other organizations were always welcome to analyse and glean the secrets of DMRC's merits and achievements. IIM Ahmedabad did find a few things—the first of them had been the organizational value and work culture in which we'd given special emphasis on timekeeping. Essentially, DMRC's responsibilities were running the trains on time and providing a convenient ambience to the riders. If the workers and employees of such an organization could not keep their time individually, collectively we believed the trains we operated would reflect the attitude. The world standard for tardiness being 3 minutes, DMRC considered 60 seconds was reason enough to record the train's arrival as late. Another value it cherished was integrity. As far as DMRC was concerned, being honest was not enough, the lofty ideals and transparency must shine through one's daily routines. A short glance at the overall work undertaken by DMRC would reveal that it had made transactions ranging in crores of rupees. Just the third phase pulled in Rs 42,000 crore. Not even a single allegation of corruption or a shred of suspicion had been alleged against DMRC. Almost all individuals and organizations associated with the Commonwealth Games had faced allegations of large-scale corruption. No one spoke against DMRC even in passing. The only reason for that was our policy of adhering to the ideals which we held on to for dear life.'

DMRC's next virtue was impeccable technical expertise. They acquired skills of an incredibly high standard by the end of the first phase. Initially, the corporation had to depend on technologies and experts from around the world. Another virtue was unflinching social commitment. The money spent by DMRC did not belong to them or to the government, but had been collected from the taxpayers, and the benefits had to reach everyone, not just a privileged few. DMRC's convictions enabled it to punch above its weight and scale the heights it did with its limited resources. The team was keen to learn lessons from their setbacks and vowed never to repeat their mistakes. Another keenly focused-on goal was to manage constructions in a manner that would minimize the inconvenience to the public. Great care was taken in ensuring the safety of the community. Barricades and safety warnings were planted. Dust and mud were not allowed to tarnish the beauty of the landscape, and roads were washed every night after the day's labour. Compensatory planting of trees was done. All this was undertaken not because someone demanded them, but voluntarily, out of a deep-rooted belief in social commitment.

Much before his time had come to step down, Sreedharan had already found his protégé. One by one, he began to transfer his extensive powers, never holding on to them longer than necessary. Like Yudhishthira from the Mahabharat, who gave up all his material possessions to set out on his great, final journey, Sreedharan passed on all the powers he had enjoyed for more than a decade without any hesitation. Letters and other official exchanges had already been addressed in the name of his successor, Manku Singh.

Sreedharan had no doubt in the continued success of DMRC as a thriving and prodigious organization even after his departure. It was but natural for anyone who had been considered the body and soul of the organization to yield to fears for its future. Some among the national media compared DMRC's situation to the forlorn state of software giant Apple whose officials were left to pick themselves up with the passing away of Steve Jobs. DMRC was an organization built over a period of fourteen years. It had accomplished much by seeing through every task it

embarked on, by not ceding an inch to negative criticism
and by not allowing itself to be swayed by the praise it
received along the way. The organization possessed the
highest level of professionalism and discipline, envied by
even the top private corporations in the country. No other
organization in the public sector could claim a comparable
professional history. The inner core of the organization and
its work culture would stand the test of time. None of its
qualities was a result of enforcement. Instead, the employees
themselves warmed up to the direction Sreedharan had
chosen for the entity. Sreedharan had professed deep faith
in the durability of the values he had introduced. As for the
world's concern about the continuation of DMRC's legacy,
Sreedharan pointed out in an interview that the core values
envisioned by Jamsetji Tata, when he laid the foundation
for the huge enterprise of the Tatas, had endured long after
his time. At DMRC too it would be the same.

As it typical in the case of high-profile bureaucrats
retiring from government service, Sreedharan too was
approached with enticing offers. The headhunters came in
droves, representing many corporate giants, domestic and
international. All they needed was a nod from him. One of
them went as far as asking him to name his own position,
and offered a salary of Rs 20 lakh a month. Sreedharan had
no interest in accepting any position anywhere. His career
had charted a blazing path and was at its tail end. His only
wish was to end the journey with his head held high. He
was past seventy-nine now. It was time to return to the
village where he had been born. Sreedharan had recognized

the traps that lay behind the alluring offers. The profit-driven corporations did not interest him; their culture was alien to him and he did not wish to find himself in the private corporate environment. Sreedharan made his views very clear, but the offers still poured in, even after he had left Delhi. Those who persisted in wooing him hoped he would change his views sooner or later. They must have been able to break down such resistance in other bureaucrats earlier. But soon they learnt that Sreedharan did not belong in that category. To be honest, has one not seen top bureaucrats in industries of strategic importance to the country, such as electronics and communications, petroleum, etc., showing no qualms in becoming even shareholders of private corporations in the same industries? It was only natural for a private company to cash in on the profile of a man who boasts an astounding professional track record and has displayed the highest integrity and moral strength in his private and public life, to help boost their own image in the market.

Though Sreedharan had categorically announced his intention to return to Kerala after retiring from DMRC, to possibly lead DMRC's projects in Kerala, some elements did not take this news well. Leaving behind DMRC and Delhi did not slow down Sreedharan's life. Pressure groups from Kerala insisted that he take over the position of chief consultant to their metro project and oversee its delivery. Earlier, KMRL wanted to do the project on its own. However, when the need arose for speedy execution, the state government had no other choice but to bring

Sreedharan into the project. Sreedharan let them know that his mere presence did not mean that the groundwork needed to build a new team and organization to expedite the process would get easier in any way. It would save a lot of time and money if DMRC were given the responsibility to deliver the new metro for Kochi. Sreedharan himself had built it from scratch. The corporation's scale of capabilities could be put to good use in Kochi. Its officers would be available at his beck and call. Only after the state government agreed to this suggestion did Sreedharan accept the position and relocate to Kerala. The responsibilities of a consultant were relatively lighter than those demanded of an executive position, but Sreedharan's presence among them would be a source of inspiration and relief to KMRL. Sreedharan's style of functioning would guarantee attention to detail.

Having taken up the new responsibility, Sreedharan routinely shuttles between Ponnani, Kochi, Kozhikode and Thiruvananthapuram. His travels outside the state have not reduced either. Recently, he was in Dubai to help finalize the third traction for the Kochi Metro.

Sreedharan could not work out of the confines of the four walls of an office in Kochi. For convenience, another office room has been set up at his home in Ponnani. Sreedharan is always on the move, and his active life has probably kept the common afflictions of his age at bay. His goal now is to put his feet up after the Kochi Metro and the monorail projects in Kozhikode and Thiruvananthapuram are done.

He has his unique views on other infrastructure projects. He says a high-speed railway system from Thiruvananthapuram to Mangalore would put Kerala in high gear for rapid development. But clouds of resistance have already gathered on the horizon. Using the most modern geo-satellites, surveys for such a line have begun, but have not been completed. There are major concerns about the widespread displacement of people and the ecological impact of it on the state, all of which nipped the plan in the bud. Sreedharan harped on the dire need for a convenient transportation system for the people and effective intervention to quell the fears and misunderstanding among the people of his state. Surveys and other efforts to develop a detailed project report for the high-speed track are still in the works, spearheaded by DMRC. Sreedharan leads this project too.

'There was never a need for large-scale relocation of people for the sake of building high-speed tracks. They need a very limited area of land. The line would steer clear of all populated areas too. In reality, only stations need some land above the ground. Train tracks could run entirely on an elevated plane above the land or through tunnels under the ground. The land owner who would allow construction over or under his property could always use his lands the way he pleases as soon as the work gets over. This kind of information has never reached the people. Hence their resistance. To help them learn more about infrastructure programmes, there must be activities such as roadshows to apprise them of the facts. Printed material could be distributed among them too. It is the duty of the government and its officers to approach the people to reassure them about their well-being and safety,' Sreedharan pointed out.

'The main objective of such a track is reduction of road traffic. For this, there is no alternative other than the expansion of railway infrastructure. There is a real chance that it may become the first ever high-speed track in the country, since states like Gujarat have only started to think about it. If we are prepared, there is no dearth of money. Japan is ready to finance the project. Their conditions are very simple. We would have to adopt their technology and machinery. I don't see anything wrong in that because they have the best and latest technology in the industry,' he said.

Talking about Kerala's long-standing gripe about being routinely overlooked in the yearly Railway Budgets, Sreedharan has a different perspective. He maintains that the people in responsible positions in Kerala never really ask for what they want. The state does not need new railway zones or workshops. The state's administration has not been able to display clarity in its demands. For that reason, the real needs of the state never get addressed. What the state needs are more tracks and trains. Electrification of the lines, doubling of the tracks and modernization of signal systems are the primary needs of the thickly populated state. More trains should run within the state and outside, connecting to the major cities in other states.

The workshops in Kerala have not been utilized optimally yet. Just see what a lot of open space in places like Shoranur remain unused, said Sreedharan, concluding that there are no projects to make use of the resources that are readily available.

The Awards

Wikipedia has a list of the top civil engineers in the world. Four from India have found place on the list, including Mokshagundam Visvesvaraya (1860–1920), the father of Indian civil engineering. Another name on the list is E. Sreedharan. On the list feature some very famous names, giving us a perspective of the august company Sreedharan shares. There is Gustav Eiffel (1832–1923), who erected the Eiffel Tower; Alexander Binny (1839–1917), who built the Blackwall Tunnel across the Thames and the Greenwich Foot Tunnel; John Bradfield (1867–1947), the creator of the Sydney Harbour Bridge and the Port Jackson Arch Bridge; and the American structural engineer William F. Bacher (b. 1953), who constructed the Burj Khalifa tower in Dubai, among others, on the list of 150 sparkling geniuses. Sir M. Visvesvaraya, the creator of massive dams, irrigation projects and flood-control systems, had also developed the Brindavan Gardens, the Mysore Sandal soap factory, and the Iron and Steel Works Company. The nation felicitated him by conferring on him the Bharat

Ratna in 1954, and made his birthday, 15 September, the national day of engineering. The massive irrigation projects he designed helped the country make gigantic leaps in agriculture and industry. There is no parallel to Sreedharan's enormous impact in the area of public transportation, ushering in a new era of rail transportation in India. In recognition of his accomplishments, awards have been coming thick and fast, both from India and overseas. The nation honoured him with the Padma Shri and Padma Bhushan awards. Union minister Pallam Raju, commending Sreedharan's genius, had said that if one were to consider his colossal contributions to the country, he would be a worthy choice for President. The demand for a Bharat Ratna for Sreedharan has been making the rounds for years now.

So far, more than sixty awards have come his way. He also has fifteen honorary doctorates. When the awards had become a routine affair, Sreedharan's secretary Govindan got curious and began to make a list of them. Recording them has become a regular chore of his. The steady stream of awards seem to be arriving in the multiples of ten—40, 50, 60, 70 and so on. Once, Sreedharan remembered five awards which were not on Govindan's list. Sreedharan's home office in Ponnani has been taken over by the awards; they fill his cupboards, tables and walls. Some of them have not even been opened. There are some more in his apartment in Bengaluru.

The first award Sreedharan received was in 1963 from the Indian Railways. Half a century later, his award score too had passed half a century. The first award was in recognition of his efforts in completing the reconstruction of the Pampan Bridge in half the scheduled time. It was a gift of Rs 1000 from the minister for railways at the time. The Padma Shri came when the first phase of the first line of the Delhi Metro was ready for inauguration in 2001. By then, the media had anointed him Metro Man. In 2008, the nation conferred the Padma Vibhushan on him, as the last extension of the first phase of the Delhi Metro was completed. At about the same time, the French government honoured him with the Chevalier de la Légion d'Honneur, and *Time* magazine named him an Asian Hero. Japan, which had the most enduring and warm relationship with Sreedharan, celebrated him with its highest honour for a civilian—the Order of the Rising Sun—towards the end of 2013. Sreedharan has many honorary doctorates—from IIT Delhi, Kurukshetra University, Rajasthan Technical University in Kota, Guru Gobind Singh Indraprastha University in Delhi, Rajiv Gandhi Proudyogiki Vishwavidyalaya in Bhopal, Cochin University of Science and Technology, Visvesvaraya Technological University in Belgaum, Singhania University in Udaipur, Jadavpur University in Kolkata, Mahamaya Technical University in Noida and Jawaharlal Nehru Technical University in Kakinada.

Sreedharan does not have any particular attachment to the awards. But from the very beginning, he felt he had reason to accept them. The money accompanying the awards would be deposited in a charity trust formed in the memory of his mother. The trust's account has accumulated a fund of over Rs 50 lakh from these awards over the last ten years. Every year, Rs 5 lakh from this fund is giving to the needy and the poor. In April, 2013, the Organization of Indian Engineers in Bahrain honoured Sreedharan with a substantial purse. Sreedharan visited Bahrain along with his wife to accept the award. In his acceptance speech to the audience, Sreedharan revealed, for the first time, how he used his gift money. He described at length the objectives and activities of the charity trust. He highlighted the changes the trust could bring to the lives of the tribal community of Karukaputhur. As soon as Sreedharan concluded his speech, a Malayalee engineer from the audience approached Sreedharan. He introduced himself as a member representing the community Sreedharan was helping. He let Sreedharan know that he too wanted to be a part of the educational and medical activities led by the trust. Sreedharan accepted his offer and told him the money he had donated would go straight into the trust and would be put to good use.

Sreedharan had spoken about the trust and its activities under his stewardship in a public forum probably only because he was in Bahrain, a foreign country where a fraternity of engineers had assembled to honour him. He had never before made even a passing reference to the trust, even in the countless speeches and interviews he had given around the nation. He believed in the conventional wisdom of being chivalrous in charity. He also believed that a portion of what he makes rightfully belonged to the poor and the downtrodden in society.

Sreedharan remembers how he set aside Rs 25,000 he had received as a token of appreciation on the completion of the Konkan project. Since the objective of the charity was primarily sustenance for the poor, it had to be in the name of his mother. It was she who had borne the brunt of poverty when it struck his family. She had great empathy for fellow humans even while she herself was in penury. The award of Rs 25,000, given in the name of Sir Mokshagundam Visvesvaraya, was the first deposit made to the charity, where Sreedharan is managing trustee. His two sons are trust members and they too contribute a part of their income to the trust. In addition to the award money, Sreedharan contributes a major portion of his own income to the trust. His entire salary from DMRC during his last four years there had been donated to the trust. He did not use even a rupee of that personally. Not too many people knew about the charity organization, Sreedharan indicated. He had been giving away 10–15 per cent of his income to the trust for years, increasing the component to 30–35 per cent, and later 100 per cent.

The regular recipient of Sreedharan's charity activities has been the tribal colony near his Karukaputhur home. The funds are mostly spent to develop public sanitation and other utilities in the area, and also to help the inhabitants to build and repair their homes. The trust funds are also used for educational and medical needs, and the purchase of school uniforms and academic supplies for the children in the neighbourhood. The education of a number of students has been entirely the trust's responsibility for some years now.

Below is the list of awards and honours that Sreedharan has received:

Awards

- *Time* magazine's Asian Hero
- Chevalier de la Légion d'Honneur from the Government of France (2005)
- The Order of the Rising Sun—Gold and Silver Star from the prime minister of Japan (2013)
- S.R. Jindal Prize
- Y.B. Chavan Award
- Om Prakash Bhasin Award for Science and Technology (2002)
- Chandrashekarananda Saraswati Prize (2002)
- CNN-IBN's Indian of the Year (2007)
- Delhi Ratna (City of Excellence) (2005)
- Bharat Shiromani Award (2005)
- National Statesman for Quality—Quimbo Award (2007)
- Excellence Award by Dr Pinnamaneni and Sita Devi Trust (2007)
- Corporate Excellence Award from the *Economic Times* (2008)
- Lifetime Achievement Award from the Institute of Company Secretaries of India (2008)

- President's Lal Bahadur Shastri National Award for Excellence in Public Administration (2008)
- Policy Change Agent for the year from the *Economic Times* (2008)
- Japan International Cooperation (JICA) Award
- IIM–J.R.D. Tata Award for Excellence in Corporate Leadership (2010)
- Ludhiana NSK Trust's Paul Mittal National Award for outstanding service to humanity (2010)
- American Biographical Institute Award
- Man of the Year Award from Mumbai Construction World (2010)
- Sir Jahangir Gandhi Award for Industrial and Social Peace (2010)
- Marthomite Syrian Church of Malabar Merit Award (2010)
- Excellence Award from Essar Steel (2011)
- Eminent Engineer Award from the *Economic Times* (2012)
- A.P. Aslam Award for brilliance (2012)
- Pratibha Samman from State Bank of Travancore, Thiruvananthapuram (2012)
- Diamond Award from Shanmukhananda Sabha in Mumbai (2012)
- AIMA Managing India Award (2012)
- For the Sake of Honour Award from the Rotary Club of Madras (2012)
- Indian Railway Service of Engineers Officers Association Award

- V. Krishnamurti Award from the Hyderabad Centre for Organizational Development
- Forbes India Leadership Award (2012)
- The India Business Leader Award from CNBC TV18 (2012)
- Sri Chithira Thirunal Award
- Excellence Award from the Satya Sai Trust
- Man of the Year Award from the Rotary Club of Calcutta (2012)
- Award from the Rotary Club of Calicut
- New Delhi Global Green Award
- Ramashramam Award
- Lifetime Achievement Award from the Bahrain Keraleeya Samajam–CET, Bahrain
- Newsmaker Award from the *Malayala Manorama* (2012)
- Amrita Television's Award for Excellence in Transportation Industry (2013)
- Vikram Sarabhai Lifetime Achievement Award from the University Grants Commission (2013)
- S.B. Joshi Memorial Award (1995)
- Person of the Year, India Vision channel
- Brahma Shah Award, Delhi (2013)
- For the Sake of Honour Award from the Rotary Club of Ernakulam
- Lokmanya Tilak Award (2013)
- Janab Tangal Kunju Musaliar Award, TKM College of Engineering, Kollam
- German Malayalee Award

- *GFiles* magazine's Lifetime Achievement Award (2013)
- South Indian Bank Award (2014)
- K.E.F. Technocrat of the Year Award, Doha, Qatar (2014)

Honorary doctorates
- IIT Delhi (2005)
- Kurukshetra University (2006)
- Doctor of Letters, Rajasthan Technical University, Kota (2009)
- Doctor of Philosophy, Guru Gobind Singh Indraprastha University, Delhi (2010)
- Doctor of Science, Rajiv Gandhi Proudyogiki Vishwavidyalaya, Bhopal (2010)
- Doctor of Letters, Cochin University of Science and Technology
- Doctor of Science, Visvesvaraya Technological University, Belgaum (2011)
- Doctor of Science, Singhania University, Udaipur
- Doctor of Literature, Jadavpur University, Kolkata
- Doctor of Philosophy, Mahamaya Technical University, Noida
- National Institute of Technology, Rourkela

Amid the Grace

If you travel a few minutes from the town of Edappal on the road to Ponnani, and take a left on to a hidden pathway, you will end up in front of a sprawling yard. Behind the large gate is a beautiful house of Victorian grandeur. The open space in front of the porch has an old iron lamp post. Flowerpots and garden sculptures adorn the walkway on either side. The big house, with its tiled roof, has the charm and attraction of a world of bygone times. The entranceway in the fence around the house has a name board titled 'Perumbayil'. When asked for permission to visit him at his house in Ponnani, Sreedharan was worried about the distance I would have to travel from Kochi. But he put me on his schedule right away. I took the road very early in the morning to keep to the scheduled time. I did not have to ask a soul to find my way there. The directions I had received from Sreedharan were perfect. As I opened the gate to let myself into the yard, Sreedharan himself came out, opening the glass door with a beaming smile. I felt the same disarming warmth I had many times before, when I used to meet Sreedharan at the DMRC office in Kochi. He had a long mark of sandalwood on his forehead, which I had not seen when he was at the office. His attire was a white dhoti and shirt, befitting the patriarch of a traditional house. Ever since his retirement from DMRC in Delhi, Sreedharan has been living in this house with his wife, Radha.

The house is Radha's inheritance from her family. The Mahalakshmi Gas Agency, owned by her brother, operates out of a corner of the plot, from where issues a constant din of vehicles and workers going about their job. The cool interior of the house, unruffled by the goings-on outside, have been furnished pleasantly. The cupboards in the visitor's room are filled with the awards and other memorabilia Sreedharan received on a regular basis. The walls are decorated with pictures of him being honoured by famous personalities from politics and industry. To the left of the entranceway is his office room. This room too abounds with his awards and gifts. In the middle of the room stands a diminutive table on which sits an old black-and-white picture of Lord Guruvayoorappan, and a wooden chair. In his capacity as chief consultant for DMRC, Sreedharan handles the daily activities of the Kochi Metro projects and the planning for the monorails from this office. DMRC official Govindan too was in the office, running it as Sreedharan's secretary. The office kicks into life every day before the clock strikes nine in the morning.

More than a century ago, a white settler had built the house. The yard around the house measured at least

three acres. Seventy-five years ago, Dr Achuthan, Radha's
father, had bought the house from the foreigner. After his
retirement from DMRC, Sreedharan had to move into the
house quite unexpectedly. Radha's aged mother then lived
alone in the house, and Sreedharan decided to shelve his
earlier plan to settle permanently in Bengaluru and headed
to Ponnani instead. After her mother's passing, since the
house belonged to Radha, circumstances dictated that they
stay put. Sreedharan's ancestral home at Karukaputhur
remained unoccupied. Until her death, his sister had
lived in that house. The house was only an hour's drive
from Ponnani. A handful of workers lived in the house
for its upkeep. Once in a week, Sreedharan would visit,
going around the house for a walk, socializing with the
neighbours and checking on the charity works in progress,
before returning to Ponnani. His preference would always
be to live in his ancestral home. But he has no plans to
move out of Ponnani at the moment, and the constant
liveliness around makes for a pleasant life in the house.

Wherever he is, Sreedharan's routine, which he has
been following for decades, does not change. Life in
Ponnani is serene and does not bear the weight of the
massive responsibilities of the offices he had occupied
earlier. For that reason, his personal routine has expanded,
becoming more elaborate. Sreedharan wakes up at 4 a.m.
every day. His morning rituals are followed by half an
hour of pranayam. He then reads the Bhagavatam for half
an hour. Believing that the Sanskrit he studied up to his
intermediate course was inadequate to take him through

the Bhagavatam and the Bhagavad Gita, he is now learning advanced Sanskrit. Govindan respectfully confirmed that 'Sreedharan Sir' was learning Sanskrit these days. Quarter past five in the morning was Sreedharan's time for half an hour of meditation. After his tea, he would watch Bhoomananda Tirtha's spiritual talk on television with his wife. This would be followed by a forty-five-minute walk with Radha. His walks, both morning and evening, are in his own yard. A walking trail has been paved through the three acres on which the house stands.

Sreedharan pointed to the walking trail from the breakfast area where we were having tea and snacks. The trail's flower beds and countryside greenery were in robust health. After the walk, a bath. Then comes catching up with the news of the day, after which Sreedharan heads to the office. Whenever at home, he would always insist that Radha join him for breakfast. He has been a committed vegetarian as far as he can remember.

Radha brought in potato sabzi, which had she fried minutes ago, and chutney for everyone at the breakfast table. The snack was accompanied by tea and sweets, which she gently prodded me to try. As she piled slices of mango on a plate, Sreedharan said the fruit had been harvested from their yard.

Reading of the Gita and the Bhagavatam resumes in the evening after work. Dinner, followed by news on television, lasts till 10 p.m. That is Sreedharan's bedtime, as it has been for years. His post-retirement schedule affords him more time for spiritual affairs, but regretfully, not as much as he thought he would get when he stepped out of DMRC. There had been an unexpected flood of new responsibilities that has followed him even here. His spiritual studies mostly consist of reading the Gita and the Bhagavatam, but he wants to delve deeper into both works. For Sreedharan, reading them has never been a mere intellectual exercise, but a process of distilling their wisdom for emulation in his own life. His library is filled with Vedic literature and the Upanishads. For some time now, he has been carrying a book on the Katha Upanishad, a word-to-word translation from the Sanskrit original by Pandit Gopalan Nair, wherever he goes. In a recent meeting, Sreedharan said he struggled to find time to read the book. Having taken up three major projects, including the metro, he is now travelling at least thrice a week to Kochi. He is also regularly on the road, travelling to at least three other destinations outside Kerala every month. Needless to say, he hardly gets time to read.

Many years ago, Sreedharan took a decision to settle down in Bengaluru. Two of his children—his daughter, Shanti, and youngest son, Krishna Das—lived there with their families. Shanti is the principal of a reputed school called Deens Academy. Her husband is a management graduate and entrepreneur. He is CEO and co-founder of the e-retail firm, Bigbasket.com. Krishna Das, who graduated from IIT Madras works for a Swedish company in Bengaluru now. Sreedharan's oldest son Ramesh lives in Chennai. After securing an MBA from Mumbai, he moved to Chennai as vice president at Tata Consultancy

Services. The third son, Dr Achutha Menon, lives in London. He studied medicine at the Government Medical College in Thiruvananthapuram, after which he did his postgraduation at Mumbai's Sion Medical College, from where he went to London for advanced studies and, having acquired a double FRCS, is now a consultant surgeon.

Sreedharan bought an apartment close to his son Krishna Das's home. He purchased it when he was about to retire from DMRC. The weather in Bengaluru was comfortably mild, and the railways' hospital was conveniently close to the apartment. This was important, for after his major heart attack in 2010, Sreedharan never missed his monthly check-ups. When it happened, he was at the Delhi airport to catch the morning flight to Kolkata. He felt an unbearable pain in his chest. He was taken to Apollo Hospital immediately. An expert panel of doctors, with Dr S.K. Gupta in the lead, treated him. The frequent check-ups that had been suggested to him are being religiously done. The choice of Bengaluru was for the sake of a comfortable life post-retirement. He had actually even moved his household articles to Bengaluru. He could have even taken care of the Kochi Metro remotely from there. That was when events took a turn in Ponnani, persuading Sreedharan and Radha to head there to take care of her mother. They stayed on.

In the middle of our conversation, Radha brought out an album of old photographs. The grand, old black-and white-photos in the album were from Sreedharan's early days in the railways. As she opened it, Sreedharan too was curious to jog his old memories. There were leaf after leaf of wedding photos, and their children's baby photos in sepia. Radha was able to recognize photographs from the different cities they had lived in, in the course of their frequent transfers. She helped Sreedharan recall the names of some of his former colleagues in Kolkata.

Sreedharan had been mentally preparing for a return to his birthplace in Kerala. More than the thrill of a second coming to his native land, he was looking forward to living a serene and quiet life of retirement, breathing the pure air of his village. He had been out of the state for most of his official life, and his mind was gradually overcome by a preoccupation to get back to the landscape of Kerala. He is past seventy-nine now. He had been working since the age of twenty-two. A ride that had begun in Bombay Port had taken him higher and higher in life, all the way to DMRC. This was the right time to halt this long and rich journey. And this remote village in Kerala, where memories and relationships that tied one through bloodlines were waiting to reconnect with him, was the right place to rest. There had been many accomplishments in his life so far, and many accolades that had come his way. There had been losses too. In a life of bound by karma, that would happen, naturally. There were many things that had been waiting to be done. The 'restful' life would be the time to recover some of the lost time. You gain some and lose some. 'I am losing the shade of an organization I'd nurtured. I am losing a number of noble colleagues who'd take my word as their command,' Sreedharan waxed eloquent in an interview he had given hours before stepping out of the DMRC office for the last time. 'It is time to go back to my village in peace. I'd spend more time on spirituality—read Bhagavatam, read Bhagavad Gita and the walks in the morning and evening and so on . . .'

Having visited many countries many times around the world, which was Sreedharan's favourite place? The question was placed out of curiosity. Could it be London, where the first metro rail was built? China, where the longest metro is furiously being completed? And, what about the extravagantly luxurious metro in Dubai? Or Tokyo, a city whose legacy of innovation and beauty laid the foundations of the Delhi Metro? How about the wealthy city of Singapore, whose many aspects of enterprise had been emulated in Sreedharan's master creation in Delhi? Sreedharan did not pause for long. 'I have travelled to most countries except South Africa and those in South America. The truth is, most countries don't have the beauty and wealth we possess in India. And, within India, there is no other place like Kerala.' He was not saying it for the sake of it. In his career spanning about five decades, he had hardly lived in Kerala. He had worked in all divisions of the railways. Responsibilities took him to destinations in and out of the country. Sreedharan was categorical—Kerala had to be god's own country. Two years had passed since he had settled in Kerala. He had never spent such a long time in the state since his school years. 'Listen, no other place in the world has purer air, water and weather. And the people here are one of a kind. Look at the stations

and trains in other places in the country. You would see
cleanliness, and trains running on schedule, in the state.
Regardless of our complaints, in terms of revenue and
passenger culture, Kerala have always been way ahead,' said
Sreedharan.

Sreedharan had liked the former chief minister of the
state E.K. Nayanar for being the consummate people's
leader he was. However, his fondness for Nayanar is also
due the rapport he felt whenever he met him. Nayanar's
simple and candid demeanour, and the way he interacted
with everyone around him, like a well-meaning patriarch,
endeared him to Sreedharan. He did not spend too much
time with Sreedharan, but whenever he did, Sreedharan
never felt otherwise.

Whenever Sreedharan made a point to him about
projects that would benefit the state and the people,
Nayanar had always paid attention, with the seriousness
it deserved. If he was convinced of a project's viability,
decisions would be made quickly. Once he made up his
mind, he would not go back on it. Sreedharan saw it
first-hand during his time with the Konkan project. The
mandate was to ensure support and coordination from all
the states involved in the project, including Kerala. There
were problems, though. The first was purely political.
Bringing together governments from the centre and the
states, who were politically in opposition, was troublesome
enough. Among the four states approached for the project,
Kerala was the only one which would not have the Konkan
passing through it. However, there was no doubt that the

biggest beneficiaries of the line would be the people of Kerala. If the state wanted to, it could have ignored the appeals for financial and material support and contributed nothing, citing the fact the line would not be built in the state. That would have been a hard argument to counter. It was knowing these facts that George Fernandes sent Sreedharan as his envoy to Kerala. Sreedharan still swears that the guaranteed cooperation from Kerala that had been extended for the project at the first meeting itself could not have happened so smoothly and decisively had it not been for Nayanar.

He was also fond of the late Madhav Rao Scindia. 'Scindia was not a Cabinet-rank minister. He was a minister of state with limited powers. Yet he ushered in considerable reforms with dedication and a willpower befitting a seasoned and adept administrator. He was the one to computerize the ticket reservation system. Scindia insisted on serving quality food to passengers on trains and at stations. He was also the minister who modernized workshops. If those reforms weren't done in his time, the state of the Indian Railways would've been undoubtedly miserable,' says Sreedharan.

Radha joined us for lunch. She took part in the conversation, which began with the journeys Sreedharan has made since accepting the Kochi Metro project; his activities as member of the state's Planning Board; the joyful get-togethers with his children and relatives; and ended with delightful trivia regarding the flower garden, the trees and the plants around the house. Sreedharan held forth on his belief system, the lifestyle he has followed since childhood and his close bond with his children.

Once more, Radha served sweets. As the empty tea cups were returned, Sreedharan suddenly said, 'To live, we only need what we have. We have more than enough. I did not even take the salary from DMRC for the last four years I've been there. It was rerouted to the trust for humanitarian projects in memory of my mother. The pension from the railways has been more than enough.' He finished his sentence and looked at Radha, as though to make sure she would agree. 'Indeed. He does think that we need only so much,' she said quietly, to which Sreedharan responded with a warm grin that filled his eyes and wrinkled the contours of his mouth.